DICTION COACH

ARIAS FOR

BASS

International Phonetic Alphabet and Diction Lessons
Recorded by a Professional, Native Speaker Coach

Diction Recordings

Corradina Caporello, Italian
Kathryn LaBouff, English
Gina Levinson, Russian
Irene Spiegelman, German
Pierre Vallet, French

International Phonetic Alphabet

Martha Gerhart, Italian and French
David Ivanov, Russian
Kathryn LaBouff, English
Irene Spiegelman, German

This Diction Coach includes all arias from *Arias for Bass* (HL50481101).
For plot notes and line-by-line translations, please see the original aria collection.

ED 4407

On the cover: "L'opéra de Paris" by Raoul Dufy
Used by permission of The Phillips Collection, Washington D.C.

ISBN 978-1-4234-1312-7

www.schirmer.com
www.halleonard.com

G. SCHIRMER, *Inc.*

DISTRIBUTED BY

HAL•LEONARD®
CORPORATION
7777 W. BLUEMOUND RD. P.O. BOX 13819 MILWAUKEE, WI 53213

PREFACE

What a wonderful opportunity for singers these volumes represent. The diction coaches recorded on the companion CDs are from the staffs of the Metropolitan Opera and The Julliard School, whose specialty is working with singers. I personally have had the opportunity to study Italian with Ms. Caporello and have experienced the sheer delight of learning operatic texts with a linguist who is devoted to the art of singing.

There are two versions of the text recorded for each aria.

1. Recitation

The Coach speaks the text of the aria as an actor would speak it, using spoken diction and capturing the mood. The guttural "R" is pronounced as in speech in French and German. Even in these free recitations, these experienced coaches are obviously informed as to how the text relates to the musical setting.

2. Diction Lessons

Dividing the text of the aria into short phrases, the coach speaks a line at a time very slowly and deliberately, without interpretation, making each word sound distinct. Time is allowed for the repetition of each phrase. In this slow version the French and German coaches adapt the guttural "R" in a manner appropriate for opera singers. The coaches in all languages make small adjustments recommended for singers in these slowly enunciated diction lessons, including elisions and liaisons between word sounds as related to the sung phrase.

There is not one universally used approach to International Phonetic Alphabet. The article before each language should be studied carefully for comprehension of the specific approach to IPA for each language in this edition.

The diction recordings can be used in many ways but a highly recommended plan is this. After carefully working regularly with the recorded diction lesson and the related IPA over several days, one should be able to reach fluency in the aria text. As an exercise separate from singing the aria, the singer should then speak the text freely, as in the diction coach's recitation. The singer likely will be inspired by the recitations recorded by the diction coaches, but after pronunciation is mastered might even begin to discover informed and individual interpretations in reciting the aria text.

By paying attention to the libretto of an aria, or an entire role, apart from the music, the opera singer can begin to understand character and interpretation in a way that would not be possible if the text is only considered by singing it. Just as an actor explores a script and a character from various historical, intellectual and emotional angles, so must the opera singer. Understanding the stated and unstated meanings of the text is fundamental in becoming a convincing actor on the opera stage, or on the opera audition stage. But the opera singer is only half done. After a thorough exploration of the words, one must discover how the composer interpreted the text and how best to express that interpretation. In great music for the opera stage, that exploration can be a fascinating lifetime journey.

Robert L. Larsen
June, 2008

CONTENTS

CD TRACK LIST
DISC ONE

		Recitation	Diction Lesson
Arias in Italian			
6	About Italian IPA		
	IL BARBIERE DI SIVIGLIA		
7	La calunnia	1	2
	LA BOHÈME		
9	Vecchia zimarra, senti	3	4
	LA CENERENTOLA		
10	Miei rampolli femminini	5	6
	DON GIOVANNI		
13	Madamina! Il catalogo è questo	7	8
	DON PASQUALE		
15	Ah! un foco insolito	9	10
	ERNANI		
16	Infelice! e tuo credevi	11	12
	LUCIA DI LAMMERMOOR		
17	Dalle stanze ove Lucia	13	14
	MACBETH		
18	Come dal ciel precipita	15	16
	LE NOZZE DI FIGARO		
19	La vendetta	17	18
21	Se vuol ballare	19	20
22	Non più andrai	21	22
24	Aprite un po' quegl'occhi	23	24
	SIMON BOCCANEGRA		
26	Il lacerato spirito	25	26
	LA SONNAMBULA		
28	Vi ravviso	27	28
	I VESPRI SICILIANI		
29	O tu, Palermo	29	30

CD TRACK LIST
DISC TWO

			Recitation	Diction Lesson
Arias in French				
	31	About French IPA		
		FAUST		
	33	Le veau d'or	1	2
	34	Vous qui faites l'endormie	3	4
		LES HUGUENOTS		
	35	Pour les couvents c'est fini (Piff, paff)	5	6
		LA JOLIE FILLE DE PERTH		
	38	Quand la flamme de l'amour	7	8
		MANON		
	39	Épouse quelque brave fille	9	10
Arias in German				
	41	About German IPA		
		DIE ENTFÜHRUNG AUS DEM SERAIL		
	44	O, wie will ich triumphiren	11	12
		DER FREISCHÜTZ		
	45	Schweig'! schweig'! damit dich niemand warnt	13	14
		DIE LUSTIGEN WEIBER VON WINDSOR		
	46	Als Büblein klein	15	16
		DIE ZAUBERFLÖTE		
	48	O Isis und Osiris	17	18
	49	In diesen heil'gen Hallen	19	20
Arias in English				
	50	About English IPA		
		THE MOTHER OF US ALL		
	52	What what is it	21	22
		STREET SCENE		
	54	Let things be like they always was	23	24
Aria in Russian				
	57	About Russian IPA		
		EUGENE ONEGIN		
	58	Gremin's Aria	25	26

ABOUT THE ITALIAN IPA TRANSLITERATIONS
by Martha Gerhart

While the IPA is currently the diction learning tool of choice for singers not familiar with the foreign languages in which they sing, differences in transliterations exist in diction manuals and on the internet, just as differences of pronunciation exist in the Italian language itself.

The Italian transliterations in this volume reflect the following choices:

All unstressed "e's" and "o's" are *closed*. This choice is based on the highest form of the spoken language, as in the authoritative Italian dictionary edited by Zingarelli. However, in practice, singers may well make individual choices as to *closed* or *open* depending upon the vocal tessitura and technical priorities.

Also, there are many Italian words (such as "sento," "cielo," and etc.) for which, in practice, both *closed* and *open* vowels in the *stressed* syllable are perfectly acceptable.

The "nasal 'm'" symbol [ɱ], indicating that the letter "n" assimilates before a "v" or an "f" (such as "inferno" becoming [im ˈfɛr no] in execution, is not used in these transliterations. This choice was a practical one to avoid confusion on the part of the student who might wonder why "in" is transcribed as if it were "im," unlike in any dictionary. However, students are encouraged to use the [ɱ] as advised by experts.

Double consonants which result, in execution, from *phrasal doubling* (*raddoppiamento sintattico*) are not transliterated as such; but students should utilize this sophistication of Italian lyric diction as appropriate.

The syllabic divisions in these transliterations are in the interest of encouraging the singer to lengthen the vowel before a single consonant rather than making an incorrect double consonant, and also to encourage the singer, when there are two consonants, the first of which is *l, m, n,* or *r*, to give more strength to the first of those two consonants.

Intervocalic "s's" are transliterated as *voiced*, despite the fact that in many words ("casa," "così," etc.) the "s" is *unvoiced* in the language (and in the above-mentioned dictionary). Preferred practice for singers is to *voice* those "s's" in the interest of legato; yet, an unvoiced "s" pronunciation in those cases is not incorrect. (*Note*: words which combine a prefix and a stem beginning with an unvoiced "s" ["risolvi," "risanare," etc.] retain the unvoiced "s" of the prefix in singing as well as in speech.)

Many Italian words have alternate pronunciations given in the best dictionaries, particularly regarding closed or open vowels. In my IPA transliterations I chose the first given pronunciation, which is not always the preferred pronunciation in common Italian usage as spoken by Corradina Caporello on the accompanying CDs. I defer to my respected colleague in all cases for her expert pronunciation of beautiful Italian diction.

Pronunciation Key

IPA Symbol	Approximate sound in English	IPA Symbol	Approximate sound in English
[i]	feet	[s]	set
[e]	potato	[z]	zip
[ɛ]	bed	[l]	lip
[a]	father	[ʎ]	million
[ɔ]	taut		
[o]	tote	[ɾ]	as *British* "very" – flipped "r"
[u]	tube	[r]	no English equivalent – rolled "r"
[j]	Yale		
[w]	watch	[n]	name
		[m]	mop
[b]	beg	[ŋ]	anchor
[p]	pet	[ɲ]	onion
[d]	deep	[tʃ]	cheese
[t]	top	[dʒ]	George
[g]	Gordon	[dz]	feeds
[k]	kit	[ts]	fits
[v]	vet		
[f]	fit	[ː]	indicates doubled consonants
[ʃ]	she	[ˈ]	indicates the primary stress; the syllable following the mark is stressed

IL BARBIERE DI SIVIGLIA

music: Gioachino Rossini

libretto: Cesare Sterbini (after *Le Barbier de Séville*, a comedy by Pierre Augustin Caron de Beaumarchais)

La calunnia

la   ka ˈlun: nja   ɛ   un   ven ti ˈtʃɛl: lo
La   calunnia   è   un   venticello,
the   slander   is   a   little wind

u na u ˈret: ta   as: ˈsa i   dʒen ˈti le
un'auretta   assai   gentile
a little breeze   very   gentle

ke   in sen ˈsi bi le   e   sot: ˈti le
che   insensibile   e   sottile,
which   imperceptible   and   subtle

led: dʒer ˈmen te   dol tʃe ˈmen te
leggermente,   dolcemente
lightly   softly

iŋ ko ˈmin tʃa   a   sus: sur ˈrar
incomincia   a   sussurrar.
begins   to   [to] whisper

ˈpja no   ˈpja no
Piano   piano,
softly   softly

ˈtɛr: ra   ˈtɛr: ra
terra terra,
close to the ground

ˈsot: to ˈvo tʃe   si bi ˈlan do
sottovoce   sibilando
in an undertone   hissing

va   skor: ˈrɛn do
va   scorrendo,
it goes   gliding

va   ron ˈdzan do
va   ronzando;
it goes   buzzing

nel: lo ˈrek: kje   ˈdel: la   ˈdʒen te
nell'orecchie   della   gente
into the ears   of the   people

sin tro ˈdu tʃe   de stra ˈmen te
s'introduce   destramente,
it slips   skillfully

e   le   ˈtɛ ste   e di   tʃer ˈvɛl: li
e   le   teste   ed i   cervelli
and   the   heads   and the   brains

fa   stor ˈdi re   e   fa   gon ˈfjar
fa   stordire   e   fa   gonfiar.
it makes   to stun   and   it makes   to inflate

ˈdal: la   ˈbok: ka   ˈfwɔ ri   uʃ: ˈʃen do
Dalla   bocca   fuori   uscendo
from the   mouth   out of   coming out

lo   skja 'mat: tso   va   kreʃ: 'ʃɛn do
lo   schiamazzo   va   crescendo;
the   uproar   goes   increasing

'prɛn de   'fɔr tsa   a   'pɔ ko   a   'pɔ ko
prende   forza   a   poco   a   poco,
it takes   force   at   little   by   little

'vo la   dʒa   di   'lɔ ko   in   'lɔ ko
vola   già   di   loco   in   loco;
it flies   now   from   place   to   place

'sem bra   il   'twɔ no
sembra   il   tuono,
it seems like   the   thunder

la   tem 'pɛ sta   ke   nel   sen
la   tempesta   che   nel   sen
the   tempest   which   in the   bosom

'del: la   fo 'rɛ sta   va   fi 'skjan do
della   foresta   va   fischiando,
of the   forest   goes   whistling

bron to 'lan do
brontolando,
rumbling

e   ti   fa   dor: 'ror   dʒe 'lar
e   ti   fa   d'orror   gelar.
and   you   it makes   with horror   to freeze

'al: la   fin   tra 'bok: ka   e   'skɔp: pja
Alla   fin   trabocca   e   scoppia,
in the   end   it overflows   and   it bursts

si pro 'pa ga   si rad: 'dop: pja
si propaga,   si raddoppia
it spreads   itself doubles

e   pro 'du tʃe   u ne splo 'zjo ne
e   produce   un'esplosione
and   it produces   an explosion

'ko me   un   'kol po   di   kan: 'no ne
come   un   colpo   di   cannone,
like   a   shot   of   cannon

un   tre 'mwɔ to   un   tem po 'ra le
un   tremuoto,   un   temporale,
an   earthquake   a   thunderstorm

un   tu 'mul to   dʒe ne 'ra le
un   tumulto   generale
a   tumult   general

ke   fa   'la rja   rim bom 'bar
che   fa   l'aria   rimbombar.
that   makes   the air   to resound

e   il   me 'ski no   ka lun: 'nja to
E   il   meschino   calunniato,
and   the   miserable   slandered one

av: vi 'li to   kal pe 'sta to
avvilito,   **calpestato,**
disgraced   *stepped on*

'sot: to il 'pub: bli ko fla 'dʒɛl: lo
sotto **il** **pubblico** **flagello**
under *the* *public* *scourge*

per gran 'sɔr te va a kre 'par
per **gran** **sorte** **va** **a** **crepar.**
through *great* *[good] fortune* *goes off* *to* *[to] die*

LA BOHÈME
music: Giacomo Puccini
libretto: Luigi Illica and Giuseppe Giacosa (after the novel *Scènes de la Vie de Bohème* by Henri Murger)

Vecchia zimarra, senti

'vɛk: kja dzi 'mar: ra 'sɛn ti
Vecchia **zimarra,** **senti,**
old *shaby coat* *hear*

'i o 'rɛ sto al pjan
io **resto** **al** **pian,**
I *remain* *on the* *ground*

tu aʃ: 'ʃen de ɾe il 'sa kro 'mon te or 'dɛ vi
tu **ascendere** **il** **sacro** **monte** **or** **devi.**
you *[to] ascend* *the* *sacred* *mountain* *now* *[you] must*

le 'mi e 'grat: tsje ri 'tʃe vi
Le **mie** **grazie** **ricevi.**
the *my* *thanks* *receive*

'ma i non kur 'va sti il 'lo go ɾo 'dor so
Mai **non** **curvasti** **il** **logoro** **dorso**
never *not* *you bowed* *the* *threadbare* *back*

'a i 'rik: ki e 'da i po 'tɛn ti
ai **ricchi** **ed ai** **potenti.**
to the *rich* *and to the* *powerful*

pas: 'sar 'nel: le 'tu e 'ta ske
Passar **nelle** **tue** **tasche**
passed *through the* *your* *pockets*

'ko me in 'an tri traŋ 'kwil: li
come **in** **antri** **tranquilli**
as if *in* *dens* *tranquil*

fi 'lɔ zo fi e po 'ɛ ti
filosofi **e** **poeti.**
philosophers *and* *poets*

'o ɾa ke i 'dʒor ni 'ljɛ ti fud: 'dʒir
Ora **che** **i** **giorni** **lieti** **fuggir,**
now *that* *the* *days* *happy* *have fled*

ti 'di ko ad: 'di o fe 'de le a 'mi ko 'mi o
ti **dico** **addio,** **fedele** **amico** **mio,**
to you *I say* *farewell* *faithful* *friend* *mine*

ad: 'di o
addio.
farewell

LA CENERENTOLA
or La Bontà in Trionfo
music: Gioachino Rossini
libretto: Jacopo Ferretti (after Charles Guillaume Etienne's libretto for *Cendrillon* by Nicolas Isouard, also after the fairy tale)

Miei rampolli femminini

ˈmjɛ i	ram ˈpolː li	femː mi ˈni ni
Miei	**rampolli**	**femminini,**
my	*offspring*	*feminine*

vi	ri ˈpu djo	mi ver ˈgoɲː ɲo
vi	**ripudio;**	**mi vergogno!**
you	*I disown*	*I am ashamed*

un	maɲː ˈɲi fi ko	ˈmi o	ˈsoɲː ɲo
Un	**magnifico**	**mio**	**sogno**
a	*magnificent*	*my*	*dream*

mi	ve ˈni ste	a	skon tʃer ˈtar
mi	**veniste**	**a**	**sconcertar.**
to me	*you came*	*to*	*[to] disrupt*

ˈko me	son	mor ti fi ˈka te
Come	**son**	**mortificate!**
how	*they are*	*mortified*

ˈdeɲː ɲe	ˈfiʎː ʎe	dun	ba ˈro ne
Degne	**figlie**	**d'un**	**barone!**
worthy	*daughters*	*of a*	*baron*

ˈvi a	si ˈlɛn tsjo	e datː ten ˈtsjo ne
Via:	**silenzio**	**ed attenzione.**
come now	*silence*	*and attention*

ˈsta te	il	ˈsoɲː ɲo	a me di ˈtar
State	**il**	**sogno**	**a meditar.**
stay	*the*	*dream*	*to [to] ponder*

mi soɲː ˈɲa i	fra	il	ˈfo sko	e il
Mi sognai	**fra**	**il**	**fosco**	**e il**
I dreamt of	*between*	*the*	*dark*	*and the*

ˈkja ɾo	un	belː ˈlisː si mo	so ˈma ɾo
chiaro	**un**	**bellissimo**	**somaro;**
light	*a*	*most beautiful*	*donkey*

un	so ˈma ɾo	ma	so ˈlɛnː ne
un	**somaro,**	**ma**	**solenne.**
a	*donkey*	*but*	*stately*

ˈkwan do	a	un	ˈtratː to
Quando	**a**	**un**	**tratto,**
when	*in*	*a*	*stroke*

o	ke	por ˈtɛn to
oh	**che**	**portento!**
oh	*what*	*wonder*

ˈsulː le	ˈspalː le	a	ˈtʃɛn to	a	ˈtʃɛn to
sulle	**spalle**	**a**	**cento**	**a**	**cento**
on the	*shoulders*	*at*	*hundred*	*by*	*hundred*

ʎi   spun ˈta va no   le   ˈpen: ne
gli   spuntavano   le   penne,
to him   appeared   the   feathers

e din   ˈa rja   ʃu   vo ˈlɔ
ed in   aria,   sciù,   volò!
and into   air   whoosh   he flew

e din   ˈtʃi ma   a   un   kam pa ˈni le
Ed in   cima   a   un   campanile
and on   top   at   a   bell-tower

ˈko me   in   ˈtrɔ no   si fer ˈmɔ
come   in   trono   si fermò.
like   on   throne   he stopped

si sen ˈti a no   per   di   ˈsot: to
Si sentiano   per   di   sotto
one could hear   through   of   below

le   kam ˈpa ne   a   din do ˈnar   din   dɔn
le   campane   a   dindonar   din,   don...
the   bells   to   [to] go ding-dong   ding   dong

kol   tʃi   tʃi   tʃu   tʃu   di ˈbɔt: to
Col   cì   cì   ciù   ciù   di botto
with the   yip   yip   yap   yap   suddenly

mi   ve ˈni ste   a   ri sveʎ: ˈʎar
mi   veniste   a   risvegliar,
to me   you came   to   [to] awaken

kol   tʃi   tʃi   tʃu   tʃu   di ˈbɔt: to
col   cì   cì   ciù   ciù   di botto
with the   yip   yip   yap   yap   suddenly

mi   fa ˈtʃe ste   ri sveʎ: ˈʎar
mi   faceste   risvegliar.
me   you made   to awaken

ma   dun   ˈsoɲ: ɲo   si   in tral ˈtʃa to
Ma   d'un   sogno   sì   intralciato
but   of a   dream   so   complicated

ˈɛk: ko   il   ˈsim bo lo   spje ˈga to
ecco   il   simbolo   spiegato.
here is   the   symbolism   explained

la   kam ˈpa na   ˈswɔ na   a ˈfɛ sta
La   campana   suona   a festa?
the   bell   rings   festively

al: le ˈgret: tsa   iŋ   ˈka za   ˈkwe sta
Allegrezza   in   casa   questa.
joy   in   house   this

ˈkwel: le   ˈpen: ne   ˈsjɛ te   ˈvo i
Quelle   penne?   Siete   voi.
those   feathers   they are   you

kwel   gran   ˈvo lo   ˈplɛ be   ad: ˈdi o
Quel   gran   volo?   Plebe   addio.
that   grand   flight   commoners   farewell

ˈrɛ sta   ˈla zi no   di ˈpɔ i
Resta   l'asino   di poi.
remains   the ass   still

12

ma	kwel:	ˈla zi no	son	ˈi o
Ma	**quell'asino**		**son**	**io,**
but	*that ass*		*[I] am*	*I*

ki	vi	ˈgwar da	ˈve de	ˈkja ɾo
chi	**vi**	**guarda**	**vede**	**chiaro**
whoever	*you*	*looks at*	*sees*	*clearly*

ke	il	so ˈma ɾo	ɛ	il	dʒe ni ˈtor
che	**il**	**somaro**	**è**	**il**	**genitor.**
that	*the*	*donkey*	*is*	*the*	*father*

fer ti ˈlis: si ma	re ˈdʒi na
Fertilissima	**regina**
most fertile	*queen*

ˈlu na	e	ˈlal tra	di ver: ˈra
l'una	**e**	**l'altra**	**diverrà;**
the one	*and*	*the other*	*will become*

e dil	ˈnɔn: no	ˈu na	dod: ˈdzi na	di	ram ˈpol: li
ed il	**nonno**	**una**	**dozzina**	**di**	**rampolli**
and the	*grandpa*	*a*	*dozen*	*of*	*offspring*

ab: brat: tʃe ˈra
abbraccierà.
will embrace

un	re	ˈpik: ko lo	di kwa	ˈsɛr vo
Un	**re**	**piccolo**	**di qua...**	**servo;**
a	*king*	*little*	*here*	*I serve*

un	re	ˈbam bo lo	di la	ˈsɛr vo
un	**re**	**bambolo**	**di là...**	**servo;**
a	*king*	*baby*	*there*	*I serve*

e	la	ˈglɔ ɾja	ˈmi a	sa ˈra	si
e	**la**	**gloria**	**mia**	**sarà,**	**sì,**
and	*the*	*glory*	*mine*	*will be*	*yes*

e dil	ˈnɔn: no	ˈu na	dod: ˈdzi na	di	ni ˈpo ti
ed il	**nonno**	**una**	**dozzina**	**di**	**nipoti**
and the	*grandpa*	*a*	*dozen*	*of*	*grandchildren*

ab: brat: tʃe ˈra
abbraccierà.
will embrace

e	la	ˈglɔ ɾja	ˈmi a	sa ˈra
e	**la**	**gloria**	**mia**	**sarà.**
and	*the*	*glory*	*mine*	*will be*

DON GIOVANNI

music: Wolfgang Amadeus Mozart

libretto: Lorenzo da Ponte (after Giovanni Bertati's libretto for Giuseppe Gazzaniga's opera *Il convitato di pietra;* also after the Don Juan legends)

Madamina! Il catalogo è questo

ma da ˈmi na   il   ka ˈta lo go   ɛ   ˈkwe sto
Madamina!   **Il**   **catalogo**   **è**   **questo**
my dear lady   *the*   *catalogue*   *is*   *this*

ˈdel: le   ˈbɛl: le   ke   a ˈmɔ   il
delle   **belle**   **che**   **amò**   **il**
of the   *beautiful women*   *whom*   *loved*   *the*

pa ˈdron   ˈmi o
padron   **mio;**
master   *mine*

un   ka ˈta lo go   ˈeʎ: ʎi   ɛ   ke   ɔ   fat: ˈti o
un   **catalogo**   **egli**   **è**   **che**   **ho**   **fatt'io;**
a   *catalogue*   *it*   *is*   *which*   *I have*   *made [I]*

os: ser ˈva te   led: ˈdʒe te   kon   me
osservate,   **leggete**   **con**   **me!**
observe   *read*   *with*   *me*

in   i ˈta lja   ˈsɛ i   ˈtʃen to   e   kwa ˈran ta
In   **Italia**   **sei**   **cento**   **e**   **quaranta,**
in   *Italy*   *six*   *hundred*   *and*   *forty*

in   al ˈmaɲ: ɲa   ˈdu e   ˈtʃen to   e   tren ˈtu na
in   **Almagna**   **due**   **cento**   **e**   **trent'una,**
in   *Germany*   *two*   *hundred*   *and*   *thirty-one*

ˈtʃen to   in   ˈfran tʃa   in   tur ˈki a   no van ˈtu na
cento   **in**   **Francia,**   **in**   **Turchia**   **novant'una;**
hundred   *in*   *France*   *in*   *Turkey*   *ninety-one*

ma   in   i ˈspaɲ: ɲa   son   dʒa   ˈmil: le   e   tre
ma,   **in**   **Ispagna**   **son**   **già**   **mille**   **e**   **tre!**
but   *in*   *Spain*   *are*   *already*   *thousand*   *and*   *three*

van   fra   ˈkwe ste   kon ta ˈdi ne
V'han   **fra**   **queste**   **contadine,**
there are   *among*   *these*   *country girls*

ka me ˈrjɛ ɾe   tʃit: ta ˈdi ne
cameriere,   **cittadine,**
chambermaids   *city girls*

van   kon ˈtes: se   ba ɾo ˈnes: se
v'han   **contesse,**   **baronesse,**
there are   *countesses*   *baronesses*

mar ke ˈza ne   prin tʃi ˈpes: se
marchesane,   **principesse,**
marquises   *princesses*

e   van   ˈdɔn: ne   ˈdoɲ: ɲi   ˈgra do
e   **v'han**   **donne**   **d'ogni**   **grado,**
and   *there are*   *women*   *of every*   *rank*

ˈdoɲ: ɲi   ˈfor ma   ˈdoɲ: ɲi   e ˈta
d'ogni   **forma,**   **d'ogni**   **età.**
of every   *form*   *of every*   *age*

'nel: la   'bjon da   'eʎ: ʎi   a   lu 'zan tsa
Nella   **bionda**   **egli**   **ha**   **l'usanza**
to the   *blond one*   *he*   *has*   *the habit*

di   lo 'dar la   la   dʒen ti 'let: tsa
di   **lodarla**   **la**   **gentilezza,**
of   *to praise in her*   *the*   *kindness*

'nel: la   'bru na   la   ko 'stan tsa
nella   **bruna**   **la**   **costanza,**
to the   *brunette*   *the*   *constancy*

'nel: la   'bjan ka   la   dol 'tʃet: tsa
nella   **bianca**   **la**   **dolcezza.**
to the   *fair-haired one*   *the*   *sweetness*

vwɔl   din 'vɛr no   la   gras: 'sɔt: ta
Vuol   **d'inverno**   **la**   **grassotta,**
he wants   *in winter*   *the*   *plump one*

vwɔl   de 'sta te   la   ma 'grɔt: ta
vuol   **d'estate**   **la**   **magrotta,**
he wants   *in summer*   *the*   *skinny one*

e   la   'gran de   ma e 'sto za
è   **la**   **grande**   **maestosa.**
and   *the*   *tall*   *imposing one*

la   pit: 'tʃi na   ɛ   oɲ: 'ɲor   vet: 'tso za
La   **piccina**   **è**   **ognor**   **vezzosa;**
the   *tiny one*   *is*   *always*   *charming*

'del: le   'vɛk: kje   fa   kon 'kwi sta
delle   **vecchie**   **fa**   **conquista,**
of the   *old ones*   *he makes*   *conquest*

pel   pja 'tʃer   di   'por le   in   'li sta
pel   **piacer**   **di**   **porle**   **in**   **lista.**
for the   *pleasure*   *of*   *to put them*   *on*   *list*

'su a   pas: 'sjon   pre do mi 'nan te
Sua   **passion**   **predominante**
his   *passion*   *predominant*

ɛ   la   'dʒo vin   prin tʃi 'pjan te
è   **la**   **giovin**   **principiante.**
is   *the*   *young*   *beginner*

non   si 'pik: ka   se   'si a   'rik: ka
Non   **si picca,**   **se**   **sia**   **ricca,**
not   *he is offended*   *if*   *she be*   *rich*

se   'si a   'brut: ta   se   'si a   'bɛl: la
se   **sia**   **brutta,**   **se**   **sia**   **bella,**
if   *she be*   *ugly*   *if*   *she be*   *beautiful*

pur 'ke   'pɔr ti   la   gon: 'nɛl: la
purchè   **porti**   **la**   **gonnella,**
as long as   *she may wear*   *the*   *skirt*

'vo i   sa 'pe te   kwel   ke   fa
voi   **sapete**   **quel**   **che**   **fa.**
you   *know*   *that*   *which*   *he does*

DON PASQUALE

music: Gaetano Donizetti
libretto: Gaetano Donizetti and Giovanni Ruffini (after the libretto by Angeli Aneli for Stefano Pavesi's *Ser Marc'Antonio*)

Ah! un foco insolito

a	un	ˈfɔ ko	in ˈsɔ li to	mi ˈsɛn to	ad: ˈdɔs: so
Ah!	**un**	**foco**	**insolito**	**mi sento**	**addosso,**
ah	*a*	*fire*	*unusual*	*I feel*	*within*

o ˈma i	re ˈzi ste ɾe	ˈi o	pju	non	ˈpɔs: so
omai	**resistere**	**io**	**più**	**non**	**posso.**
now	*to resist*	*I*	*more*	*not*	*[I] am able*

del: le ˈta	ˈvɛk: kja	ˈskɔr do	i	ma ˈlan: ni
Dell'età	**vecchia**	**scordo**	**i**	**malanni,**
of the age	*old*	*I forget*	*the*	*woes*

mi ˈsɛn to	ˈdʒo vi ne	ˈko me	a	ven ˈtan: ni
mi sento	**giovine**	**come**	**a**	**vent'anni.**
I feel	*young*	*like*	*at*	*twenty years*

dɛ	ˈka ɾa	af: ˈfret: ta ti
Deh!	**cara,**	**affrettati!**
please	*dear one*	*hurry*

ˈvjɛ ni	spo ˈzi na
Vieni,	**sposina!**
come	*little bride*

ˈɛk: ko	di	ˈbam bo li	ˈmɛd: dza	dod: ˈdzi na
Ecco,	**di**	**bamboli**	**mezza**	**dozzina**
here	*of*	*children*	*half*	*dozen*

dʒa	ˈveg: go	ˈnaʃ: ʃe ɾe	ˈkreʃ: ʃe ɾe
già	**veggo**	**nascere,**	**crescere,**
already	*I see*	*to be born*	*to grow*

a	me	din ˈtor no	ˈveg: go	sker ˈtsar
a	**me**	**d'intorno**	**veggo**	**scherzar.**
at	*me*	*all around*	*I see*	*to play*

ˈvjɛ ni	ke	un	ˈfɔ ko	in ˈsɔ li to
Vieni,	**chè**	**un**	**foco**	**insolito**
come	*because*	*a*	*fire*	*unusual*

mi ˈsɛn to	ad: ˈdɔs: so
mi sento	**addosso,**
I feel	*within*

o	ˈka sko	ˈmɔr to	kwa
o	**casco**	**morto**	**qua.**
or	*I fall*	*dead*	*here*

dɛ	ˈvjɛ ni	af: ˈfret: ta ti	ˈbɛl: la	spo ˈzi na
Deh!	**vieni,**	**affrettati,**	**bella**	**sposina!**
please	*come*	*hurry*	*beautiful*	*little bride*

dʒa	di	ˈbam bo li	ˈmɛd: dza	dod: ˈdzi na
Già	**di**	**bamboli**	**mezza**	**dozzina**
already	*of*	*children*	*half*	*dozen*

a	me	din ˈtor no	ˈveg: go	sker ˈtsar
a	**me**	**d'intorno**	**veggo**	**scherzar.**
at	*me*	*all around*	*I see*	*to play*

ERNANI

music: Giuseppe Verdi

libretto: Francesco Maria Piave (after Victor Hugo's play *Hernani*)

Infelice! e tuo credevi

ke	'ma i	ved: 'dʒi o
Che	**mai**	**vegg'io!**
what	*ever*	*see I*

nel	pe ne 'tral	pju	'sa kro	di	'mi a	ma 'dʒo ne
Nel	**penetral**	**più**	**sacro**	**di**	**mia**	**magione;**
in the	*innermost part*	*most*	*sacred*	*of*	*my*	*dwelling*

'prɛs: so	a	'lɛ i	ke	'spɔ za	'ɛs: ser	do 'vra
presso	**a**	**lei,**	**che**	**sposa**	**esser**	**dovrà**
near	*to*	*her*	*who*	*bride*	*to be*	*will ought*

dun	'sil va
d'un	**Silva,**
of a	*Silva*

'du e	se dut: 'to ri	'i o	'skɔr go
due	**seduttori**	**io**	**scorgo?**
two	*seducers*	*I*	*[I] sight*

en 'tra te	o 'la	'mjɛ i	'fi di	ka va 'ljɛ ri
Entrate,	**olà,**	**miei**	**fidi**	**cavalieri.**
enter	*hello there*	*my*	*faithful*	*cavaliers*

'si a	oɲ: 'ɲun	te sti 'mɔn	del	di zo 'no re
Sia	**ognun**	**testimon**	**del**	**disonore,**
let be	*each*	*witness*	*of the*	*dishonor*

del: 'lon ta	ke	si 'rɛ ka	al
dell'onta	**che**	**si reca**	**al**
of the shame	*which*	*is brought*	*to the*

'su o	siɲ: 'ɲo re
suo	**signore.**
his	*master*

in fe 'li tʃe	e	'tu o	kre 'de vi	si	bɛl
Infelice!	**e**	**tuo**	**credevi**	**sì**	**bel**
unhappy one	*and*	*yours*	*you believed*	*so*	*beautiful*

'dʒiʎ: ʎo	im: ma ko 'la to
giglio	**immacolato!**
lily	*spotless*

del	'tu o	'kri n	fra	le	'ne vi
Del	**tuo**	**crine**	**fra**	**le**	**nevi**
on the	*your*	*head of hair*	*among*	*the*	*snows*

'pjom ba	in 've tʃe	il	di zo 'nor
piomba	**invece**	**il**	**disonor.**
falls	*instead*	*the*	*dishonor*

a	per 'ke	le 'ta de	in	'se no
Ah,	**perché**	**l'etade**	**in**	**seno**
ah	*why*	*the age*	*in*	*breast*

'dʒo vin	'kɔ re	ma	ser 'ba to
giovin	**core**	**m'ha**	**serbato!**
young	*heart*	*for me has*	*preserved*

mi   do ˈve van   ʎi   ˈanː ni al ˈme no
Mi   dovevan   gli   anni   almeno
for me   [they] had ought the   years   at least

far   di ˈdʒe lo aŋ ˈko ɾa il   kɔr
far   di gelo   ancora   il   cor.
to make of   ice   yet   the   heart

LUCIA DI LAMMERMOOR
music: Gaetano Donizetti
libretto: Salvatore Commarano (after Walter Scott's novel *The Bride of Lammermoor*)

Dalle stanze ove Lucia

ˈtʃɛsː si a   ˈtʃɛsː si kwel kon ˈtɛn to
Cessi,   ah   cessi   quel   contento.
cease   ah   cease   that   pleasure

ˈtʃɛsː si ˈtʃɛsː si un   ˈfjɛ ɾo e ˈvɛn to
Cessi,   cessi... Un   fiero   evento!
cease   cease   a   cruel   event

a
Ah!
ah

ˈdalː le ˈstan tse ˈo ve lu ˈtʃi a
Dalle   stanze   ove   Lucia
from the rooms   to which Lucia

ˈtratː ta a ˈve a kol ˈsu o kon ˈsɔr te
tratta   avea   col   suo   consorte,
gone into had   with the her   consort

un la ˈmen to un ˈgri do uʃː ˈʃi a
un   lamento... un   grido   uscia,
a   lament   a   cry   came out

ˈko me dwɔm vi ˈtʃi no a ˈmɔr te
come   d'uom   vicino   a   morte!
like   of man   near   to   death

ˈkor si ˈratː to iŋ ˈkwelː le ˈmu ɾa
Corsi   ratto   in   quelle   mura...
I ran   quickly to   those   walls

ˈa i terː ˈri bi le ʃa ˈgu ɾa
ahi!   terribile   sciagura!
alas   terrible   disaster

ˈste zo ar ˈtu ɾo al swɔl dʒa ˈtʃe va
Steso   Arturo   al   suol   giaceva
outspread Arturo   on the floor   was lying

ˈmu to ˈfredː do in saŋ gwi ˈna to
muto,   freddo,   insanguinato!
silent   cold   bloody

e lu ˈtʃi a latː ˈtʃar strin ˈdʒe va
e Lucia   l'acciar   stringeva,
and Lucia   the blade was clutching

ke fu dʒa del tru tʃi ˈda to
che fu già del trucidato!
which was formerly from the slain one

ˈelː la in me le ˈlu tʃi afː ˈfisː se
Ella in me le luci affisse.
she on me the eyes fixed

il ˈmi o ˈspɔ zo o ˈvɛ mi ˈdisː se
« Il mio sposo ov'è? » mi disse,
the my husband where he is to me she said

e nel ˈvol to ˈsu o palː ˈlɛn te
e nel volto suo pallente
and on the face hers pale

un sorː ˈri zo ba le ˈnɔ
un sorriso balenò!
a smile flashed

in fe ˈli tʃe ˈdelː la ˈmen te la vir ˈtu de
Infelice! della mente la virtude
unhappy one of the mind the power

a ˈlɛ i maŋ ˈkɔ a
a lei mancò! ah!
to her lacked ah

a ˈkwelː la ˈdɛ stra di ˈsaŋ gwe im ˈpu ɾa
Ah! quella destra di sangue impura
ah that [right] hand with blood impure

ˈli ɾa non ˈkja mi su ˈno i del tʃɛl
l'ira non chiami su noi del ciel.
the anger not may call upon us of the heaven

MACBETH

music: Giuseppe Verdi

libretto: Francesco Maria Piave (after the tragedy by William Shakespeare)

Come dal ciel precipita

ˈstu dja il ˈpasː so o ˈmi o ˈfiʎː ʎo
Studia il passo, o mio figlio!
study the step o my son

uʃː ˈʃam da ˈkwe ste te ˈnɛ bre
Usciam da queste tenebre;
let us go out from these darknesses

un ˈsɛn so iɲː ˈɲɔ to ˈnaʃː ʃer mi ˈsɛn to
un senso ignoto nascer mi sento
a feeling unknown to be born I feel

in ˈpɛtː to
in petto,
in breast

ˈpjɛn di ˈtri sto pre ˈza dʒo
pien di tristo presagio
full of sad presentiment

'e   di   so 'spɛt: to
e   di   sospetto.
and   of   suspicion

'ko me   dal   tʃɛl   pre 'tʃi pi ta   'lom bra
Come   dal   ciel   precipita   l'ombra
how   from the   sky   precipitates   the shadow

pju   'sɛm pre   o 'sku ɾa
più   sempre   oscura!
more   always   gloomy

in   'nɔt: te   u 'gwal   tra 'fis: se ɾo   duŋ 'ka no
In   notte   ugual   trafissero   Duncano,
on   night   like   they slew   Duncan

il   'mi o   siɲ: 'ɲor
il   mio   signor.
the   my   lord

'mil: le   af: fan: 'no ze   im: 'ma dʒi ni
Mille   affannose   immagini
thousand   troubling   images

man: 'nun tʃa no   zven 'tu ɾa
m'annunciano   sventura,
to me they foretell   misfortune

e   il   'mi o   pen 'sjɛ ɾo   iŋ 'gom bra no
e   il   mio   pensiero   ingombrano
and   the   my   thought   they encumber

di   'lar ve   e   di   ter: 'ror
di   larve   e   di   terror.
with   phantoms   and   with   terror

LE NOZZE DI FIGARO

music: Wolfgang Amadeus Mozart

libretto: Lorenzo da Ponte (after *La Folle Journée, ou Le Mariage de Figaro*, a comedy by Pierre Augustin Caron de Beaumarchais)

La vendetta

'bɛ ne   'i o   'tut: to   fa 'rɔ
Bene,   io   tutto   farò;
fine   I   everything   [I] will do

'sɛn tsa   ri 'zɛr ve
senza   riserve,
without   reservations

'tut: to   a   me   pa le 'za te
tutto   a   me   palesate.
everything   to   me   disclose

a 'vrɛ i   pur   'gu sto   di   dar   in   'moʎ: ʎe
(Avrei   pur   gusto   di   dar   in   moglie
I should have   certainly   pleasure   in   giving   as   wife

la   'mi a   'sɛr va   an 'ti ka   a   ki
la   mia   serva   antica   a   chi
the   my   servant   old   to   one who

mi	'fe tʃe	un	di	ra 'pir	la 'mi ka
mi	**fece**	**un**	**dì**	**rapir**	**l'amica.)**
from me	*did*	*one*	*day*	*[to] steal*	*the girlfriend*

la	ven 'det: ta	o	la	ven 'det: ta
La	**vendetta,**	**oh,**	**la**	**vendetta**
the	*vengeance*	*oh*	*the*	*vengeance*

ɛ	un	pja 'tʃer	ser 'ba to	'a i	'sad: dʒi
è	**un**	**piacer**	**serbato**	**ai**	**saggi.**
is	*a*	*pleasure*	*reserved*	*for the*	*wise ones*

lob: bli 'ar	'lon te	ʎi	ol 'trad: dʒi
L'obbliar	**l'onte,**	**gli**	**oltraggi**
the forgetfulness	*the disgraces*	*the*	*offences*

ɛ	bas: 'set: tsa	ɛ	oɲ: 'ɲor	vil 'ta
è	**bassezza,**	**è**	**ognor**	**viltà.**
is	*baseness*	*is*	*always*	*cowardice*

kol: la 'stut: tsja	kol: lar 'gut: tsja
Coll'astuzia,	**coll'arguzia,**
with the shrewdness	*with the wit*

kol	dʒu 'dit: tsjo	kol	kri 'tɛ ɾjo
col	**giudizio,**	**col**	**criterio,**
with the	*wisdom*	*with the*	*good sense*

si po 'trɛb: be
si potrebbe...
one would be able

il	'fat: to	ɛ	'sɛ ɾjo
il	**fatto**	**è**	**serio.**
the	*matter*	*is*	*serious*

ma	kre 'de te	si fa 'ra
Ma	**credete,**	**si farà.**
but	*believe*	*it will be done*

se	'tut: to	il	'kɔ di tʃe	do 'ves: si
Se	**tutto**	**il**	**codice**	**dovessi**
if	*all*	*the*	*[legal] code*	*I should have had to*

'vɔl dʒe ɾe
volgere,
[to] bend

se	'tut: to	'lin di tʃe	do 'ves: si	'lɛd: dʒe ɾe
se	**tutto**	**l'indice**	**dovessi**	**leggere,**
if	*all*	*the index*	*I should have had to*	*[to] read*

kon	un	e 'kwi vo ko	kon	un	si 'nɔ ni mo
con	**un**	**equivoco,**	**con**	**un**	**sinonimo**
with	*an*	*ambiguity*	*with*	*a*	*synonym*

'kwal ke	gar 'buʎ: ʎo	si tro ve 'ra
qualche	**garbuglio**	**si troverà.**
some	*confusion*	*will be found*

'tut: ta	si 'viʎ: ʎa	ko 'noʃ: ʃe	'bar to lo
Tutta	**Siviglia**	**conosce**	**Bartolo—**
all	*Seville*	*knows*	*Bartolo*

il	'bir bo	'fi ga ɾo	'vin to	sa 'ra
il	**birbo**	**Figaro**	**vinto**	**sarà.**
the	*rascal*	*Figaro*	*defeated*	*will be*

Se vuol ballare

'bra vo   siɲː ɲor   pa 'dro ne
Bravo,   **signor**   **padrone!**
good for you   *sir*   *master*

'o ɾa   iŋ ko 'min tʃo   a ka 'pir   il   mi 'stɛ ro
Ora   **incomincio**   **a** **capir** **il** **mistero,**
now   *I begin*   *to* *understand* *the* *mystery*

e   a   ve 'der   'skjeːто
e   **a**   **veder**   **schietto**
and *to* *[to] see* *frankly*

'tutː to   il   'vɔ stro   pro 'dʒɛtː to
tutto   **il**   **vostro**   **progetto;**
all   *the* *your*   *plan*

a   'lon dra   ɛ   've ɾo
a   **Londra,**   **è**   **vero?**
to *London* *it is* *true*

'vo i   mi 'ni stro   'i o   korː 'rjɛ ɾo
Voi   **ministro,**   **io**   **corriero,**
you *minister* *I*   *courier*

e   la   su 'zanː na
e   **la**   **Susanna...**
and *the* *Susanna*

se 'kre ta   am baʃː ʃa 'tri tʃe
secreta   **ambasciatrice.**
secret   *ambassadress*

non   sa 'ɾa   'fi ga ɾo   il   'di tʃe
Non   **sarà,**   **Figaro**   **il**   **dice!**
not *it will be* *Figaro* *it* *says*

se   vwɔl   balː 'la ɾe   siɲː ɲor   kon 'ti no
Se   **vuol**   **ballare,**   **signor**   **contino,**
if *you want* *to dance* *sir*   *dear count*

il   ki tarː 'ri no   le   swo ne 'ɾɔ   si
il   **chitarrino**   **le**   **suonerò,**   **sì.**
the *guitar*   *for you* *I will play* *yes*

se   vwɔl   ve 'ni ɾe   'nelː la   'mi a   'skwɔ la
Se   **vuol**   **venire**   **nella**   **mia**   **scuola,**
if *you want* *to come* *to the* *my* *school*

la   ka pri 'ɔ la   le   in seɲ ɲe 'ɾɔ   si
la   **capriola**   **le**   **insegnerò,**   **sì.**
the *caper*   *to you* *I will teach* *yes*

sa 'prɔ   ma   'pja no
Saprò,   **ma**   **piano;**
I will know how *but* *slowly*

'mɛʎː ʎo   'oɲː ɲi   ar 'ka no   disː si mu 'lan do
meglio   **ogni**   **arcano**   **dissimulando**
better *every* *secret* *dissimulating*

sko 'prir   po 'trɔ
scoprir   **potrò.**
to discover *I will be able*

'lar te   sker 'mɛn do   'lar te   a do 'pran do
L'arte   **schermendo,**   **l'arte**   **adoprando,**
the cunning   *defending*   *the cunning*   *using*

di   kwa   pun 'dʒen do   di   la   sker 'tsan do
di   **quà**   **pungendo,**   **di**   **là**   **scherzando,**
from   *here*   *stinging*   *from*   *there*   *joking*

'tut: te   le   'mak: ki ne   ro veʃ: ʃe 'rɔ
tutte   **le**   **macchine**   **rovescierò.**
all   *the*   *plots*   *I will turn upside down*

Non più andrai

non   pju   an 'dra i   far fal: 'lo ne   a mo 'ro zo
Non   **più**   **andrai,**   **farfallone**   **amoroso,**
not   *more*   *you will go*   *big butterfly*   *amorous*

'nɔt: te   e   'dʒor no   din 'tor no   dʒi 'ran do
notte   **e**   **giorno**   **d'intorno**   **girando,**
night   *and*   *day*   *all around*   *circling*

'del: le   'bɛl: le   tur 'ban do   il   ri 'pɔ zo
delle   **belle**   **turbando**   **il**   **riposo,**
of the   *beautiful women*   *disturbing*   *the*   *repose*

nar tʃi 'zet: to   a don 'tʃi no   da 'mor
Narcisetto,   **Adoncino**   **d'amor.**
little Narcissus   *little Adonis*   *of love*

non   pju   a 'vra i   'kwe sti   'bɛ i   pen: nak: 'ki ni
Non   **più**   **avrai**   **questi**   **bei**   **pennacchini,**
not   *more*   *you will have*   *these*   *beautiful*   *feathers*

kwel   kap: 'pɛl: lo   led: 'dʒe ɾo   e   ɡa 'lan te
quel   **cappello**   **leggiero**   **e**   **galante,**
that   *hat*   *light*   *and*   *gallant*

'kwel: la   'kjɔ ma   kwel 'laɾ ja   bril: 'lan te
quella   **chioma,**   **quell'aria**   **brillante,**
that   *hair*   *that air*   *sparkling*

kwel   ver 'miʎ: ʎo   don: 'ne sko   ko 'lor
quel   **vermiglio**   **donnesco**   **color!**
that   *vermillion*   *womanish*   *color*

non   pju   a 'vra i   'kwe i   pen: nak: 'ki ni
Non   **più**   **avrai**   **quei**   **pennacchini,**
not   *more*   *you will have*   *those*   *feathers*

kwel   kap: 'pɛl: lo   'kwel: la   'kjɔ ma
quel   **cappello,**   **quella**   **chioma,**
that   *hat*   *that*   *hair*

kwel: 'la ɾja   bril: 'lan te
quell'aria   **brillante!**
that air   *sparkling*

tra   ɡwer: 'rjɛ ɾi   pof: far 'bak: ko
Tra   **guerrieri,**   **poffar Bacco!**
among   *warriers*   *amazing Bacchus = "by Jove"*

gran   mu 'stak: ki   'stret: to   'sak: ko
Gran   **mustacchi,**   **stretto**   **sacco,**
big   *whiskers*   *tight*   *tunic*

'skjɔp: po   in   'spal: la   'ʃa bla   al   'fjaŋ ko
schioppo   in   spalla,   sciabla   al   fianco,
rifle   on   shoulder   sabre   at the   hip

'kɔl: lo   'drit: to   'mu zo   'fraŋ ko
collo   dritto,   muso   franco,
neck   straight   face   straightforward

un   gran   'ka sko   o   un   gran   tur 'ban te
un   gran   casco,   o   un   gran   turbante,
a   big   helmet   or   a   big   turban

'mol to   o 'nor   'pɔ ko   kon 'tan te
molto   onor,   poco   contante.
much   honor   little   cash

e din 've tʃe   del   fan 'daŋ go
Ed invece   del   fandango
and instead   of the   fandango

'u na   'mar tʃa   per   il   'faŋ go
una   marcia   per   il   fango.
a   march   through   the   mud

per   mon 'taɲ: ɲe   per   val: 'lo ni
Per   montagne,   per   valloni,
over   mountains   through   ravines

kon   le   'ne vi   e   i   sol: li 'o ni
con   le   nevi,   e   i   sollioni,
with   the   snows   and   the   summer heats

al   kon 'tʃɛr to   di   trom 'bo ni   di   bom 'bar de
al   concerto   di   tromboni,   di   bombarde,
to the   chorus   of   trombones   of   bombards

di   kan: 'no ni   ke   le   'pal: le
di   cannoni,   che   le   palle
of   cannons   which   the   cannonballs

in   'tut: ti   i   'twɔ ni
in   tutti   i   tuoni,
in   all   the   thunder

al: lo 'rek: kjo   fan   fi 'skjar
all'orecchio   fan   fischiar.
in the ear   make   to whistle

ke ɾu 'bi no   'al: la   vit: 'tɔ ɾja
Cherubino,   alla   vittoria,
Cherubino   to the   victory

'al: la   'glɔ ɾja   mi li 'tar
alla   gloria   militar!
to the   glory   military

Aprite un po' quegl'occhi

'tut: to   ε   di 'spo sto
Tutto   è   disposto;
everything   is   prepared

'lo ɾa   do 'vrɛb: be   'ɛs: ser   vi 't∫i na
l'ora   dovrebbe   esser   vicina.
the hour   ought   to be   near at hand

'i o   'sɛn to   'dʒɛn te   ε   'des: sa
Io   sento   gente...   è   dessa!
I   [I] hear   people   it is   she

non   ε   al 'kun
Non   è   alcun;
not   it is   anyone

'bu ja   ε   la   'nɔt: te
buja   è   la   notte,
dark   is   the   night

e 'di o   ko 'min t∫o   o 'ma i   a   'fa ɾe
ed io   comincio   omai   a   fare
and I   [I] begin   now   to   [to] do

il   ∫i mu 'ni to   me 'stjɛ ɾe   di   ma 'ri to
il   scimunito   mestiere   di   marito.
the   silly   job   of   husband

iŋ 'gra ta   nel   mo 'men to   'del: la   'mi a
Ingrata!   Nel   momento   della   mia
ungrateful one   in the   moment   of the   my

t∫e ɾi 'mɔ nja   'e i   go 'de va   led: 'dʒɛn do
cerimonia   ei   godeva   leggendo;
ceremony   he   was enjoying   reading

e   nel   ve 'der lo   'i o   ri 'de va   di
e   nel   vederlo,   io   rideva   di
and   in the   seeing him   I   was laughing   at

me   'sɛn tsa   sa 'per lo
me   senza   saperlo.
myself   without   knowing it

o   su 'zan: na   'kwan ta   'pe na   mi   'kɔ sti
O   Susanna!   quanta   pena   mi   costi!
oh   Susanna   how much   pain   me   you cost

kon   kwel: lin 'dʒɛ nu a   'fat: t∫a
Con   quell'ingenua   faccia,
with   that ingenuous   face

kon   kweʎ: 'ʎɔk: ki   in: no 't∫ɛn ti
con   quegl'occhi   innocenti,
with   those eyes   innocent

ki   kre 'du to   la 'vri a
chi   creduto   l'avria?
who   believed   it would have

a   ke   il   fi 'dar si   a   'dɔn: na
Ah!   che   il   fidarsi   a   donna
ah   that   the   placing one's trust   in   woman

ɛ   oɲː ˈɲor   folː ˈli a
è   ognor   follia.
is   always   folly

a ˈpri te   un   pɔ   kweʎː ˈʎɔkː ki
Aprite   un   po'   quegl'occhi,
open   a   little   those eyes

ˈwɔ mi ni   iŋ ˈka u ti   e   ˈʃɔkː ki
uomini   incauti   e   sciocchi.
men   incautious   and   foolish

gwar ˈda te   ˈkwe ste   ˈfemː mi ne
Guardate   queste   femmine,
look at   these   females

gwar ˈda te   ˈkɔ za   son
guardate   cosa   son!
look at   what   [they] are

ˈkwe ste   kja ˈma te   ˈdɛ e   ˈdaʎː ʎi   iŋ ganː ˈna ti
Queste   chiamate   dee,   dagli   ingannati
these   you call   goddesses   from the   deceived

ˈsɛn si   a   ˈku i   tri ˈbu ta   in ˈtʃɛn si
sensi,   a   cui   tributa   incensi
senses   on   whom   bestows   adulations

la   ˈde bo le   ra ˈdʒon
la   debole   ragion.
the   weak   reason

son   ˈstre ge   ke   iŋ ˈkan ta no
Son   streghe   che   incantano
they are   witches   who   charm

per   ˈfar tʃi   pe ˈnar
per   farci   penar,
for   to make us   [to] suffer

si ˈrɛ ne   ke   ˈkan ta no
sirene   che   cantano
sirens   who   sing

per   ˈfar tʃi   afː fo ˈgar
per   farci   affogar,
for   to make us   [to] drown

tʃi ˈvetː te   ke   alː ˈlɛtː ta no
civette   che   allettano
owls   that   allure

per   ˈtrar tʃi   le   ˈpju me
per   trarci   le   piume,
for   to pull from us   the   feathers

ko ˈme te   ke   ˈbrilː la no
comete   che   brillano
comets   which   glitter

per   ˈtɔʎː ʎer tʃi   il   ˈlu me
per   toglierci   il   lume;
for   to take away from us   the   light

son   'rɔ ze   spi 'no ze
son   **rose**   **spinose,**
they are   *roses*   *thorny*

son   'vol pi   vet: 'tso ze
son   **volpi**   **vezzose,**
they are   *foxes*   *graceful*

son   'or se   be 'niɲ: ɲe
son   **orse**   **benigne,**
they are   *she-bears*   *gentle*

ko 'lom be   ma 'liɲ: ɲe
colombe   **maligne,**
doves   *malicious*

ma 'ɛs tre   diŋ 'gan: ni
maestre   **d'inganni,**
masters   *of deceptions*

a 'mi ke   daf: 'fan: ni
amiche   **d'affanni,**
friends   *of anguishes*

ke   'fiŋ go no   'mɛn to no
che   **fingono,**   **mentono.**
who   *pretend*   *lie*

a 'mo ɾe   non   'sɛn ton   non
Amore   **non**   **senton,**   **non**
love   *not*   *they feel*   *not*

      'sɛn ton   pje 'ta   nɔ
      senton   **pietà,**   **no.**
      they feel   *pity*   *no*

il   'rɛ sto   nol   'di ko
Il   **resto**   **nol**   **dico,**
the   *rest*   *not it*   *I say*

dʒa   oɲ: 'ɲu no   lo   sa
già   **ognuno**   **lo**   **sa.**
already   *each man*   *it*   *knows*

SIMON BOCCANEGRA

music: Giuseppe Verdi
libretto: Francesca Maria Piave and Arrigo Boito

Il lacerato spirito

a   te   le 'strɛ mo   ad: 'di o
A   **te**   **l'estremo**   **addio,**
to   *you*   *the final*   *farewell*

pa 'la dʒo   al 'tɛ ɾo
palagio   **altero,**
palace   *proud*

'fred: do   se 'pol kro   del: 'lan dʒo lo   'mi o
freddo   **sepolcro**   **dell'angiolo**   **mio!**
cold   *sepulchre*   *of the angel*   *mine*

ne	a	pro 'ted: dʒer lo	'val si
Nè	**a**	**proteggerlo**	**valsi!**
not	*to*	*[to] protect her*	*I was not of use*

o	ma le 'det: to
Oh	**maledetto!**
oh	*cursed one*

o	'vi le	se dut: 'to ɾe
Oh	**vile**	**seduttore!**
oh	*vile*	*seducer*

e	tu,	'ver dʒin	sof: 'fri sti	ra 'pi ta
E	**tu,**	**Vergin,**	**soffristi**	**rapita**
and	*you*	*Virgin*	*you allowed*	*robbed*

a	'lɛ i	la	ver dʒi 'nal	ko 'ro na
a	**lei**	**la**	**verginal**	**corona?**
from	*her*	*the*	*virginal*	*crown*

a	ke	'dis: si	de 'li ɾo
Ah!	**che**	**dissi?**	**deliro!**
ah	*what*	*I said*	*I rave*

a	mi	per 'do na
Ah!	**mi**	**perdona!**
ah	*me*	*forgive*

il	la tʃe 'ra to	'spi ɾi to
Il	**lacerato**	**spirito**
the	*lacerated*	*spirit*

del	'mɛ sto	dʒe ni 'to ɾe
del	**mesto**	**genitore**
of the	*sad*	*father*

'ɛ ɾa	ser 'ba to	a	'strat: tsjo
era	**serbato**	**a**	**strazio**
was	*reserved*	*for*	*agony*

din 'fa mja	e	di	do 'lo ɾe
d'infamia	**e**	**di**	**dolore.**
of infamy	*and*	*of*	*sorrow*

il	'sɛr to	a	'lɛ i	de	'mar ti ɾi
Il	**serto**	**a**	**lei**	**de'**	**martiri**
the	*wreath*	*to*	*her*	*of [the]*	*martyrs*

pje 'to zo	il	'tʃɛ lo	djɛ
pietoso	**il**	**cielo**	**diè.**
mercifully	*the*	*heaven*	*gave*

're za	al	ful 'gor	'deʎ: ʎi	'an dʒe li
Resa	**al**	**fulgor**	**degli**	**angeli,**
returned	*to the*	*radiance*	*of the*	*angels*

'prɛ ga	ma 'ri a	per	me
prega,	**Maria,**	**per**	**me.**
pray	*Maria*	*for*	*me*

LA SONNAMBULA

music: Vincenzo Bellini
libretto: Felice Romani (after *La Sonnambule,* a ballet-pantomime by Eugène Scribe)

Vi ravviso

il	mu 'li no	il	'fon te	il	'bɔ sko
Il	**mulino...**	**il**	**fonte...**	**il**	**bosco...**
the	*mill*	*the*	*fountain*	*the*	*woods*

e	vi 'tʃin	la	fat: to 'ri a
e	**vicin**	**la**	**fattoria!**
and	*nearby*	*the*	*farmhouse*

vi	rav: 'vi zo	o	'lwɔ gi	a 'mɛ ni
Vi	**ravviso,**	**o**	**luoghi**	**ameni,**
you	*I recognize*	*o*	*places*	*pleasant*

iŋ	'ku i	'ljɛ ti	iŋ	'ku i	se 're ni
in	**cui**	**lieti,**	**in**	**cui**	**sereni**
in	*which*	*happy*	*in*	*which*	*serene*

si	traŋ 'kwil: lo	i	di	pas: 'sa i
sì	**tranquillo**	**i**	**dì**	**passai**
so	*peaceful*	*the*	*days*	*I passed*

'del: la	'pri ma	dʒo ven 'tu
della	**prima**	**gioventù!**
of the	*first*	*youth*

'ka ɾi	'lwɔ gi	'i o	vi	tro 'va i
Cari	**luoghi,**	**io**	**vi**	**trovai,**
dear	*places*	*I*	*you*	*I found*

ma	kwel	di	non	'trɔ vo	pju
ma	**quei**	**dì**	**non**	**trovo**	**più!**
but	*those*	*days*	*not*	*I find*	*more*

ma	fra	'vo i	se	non	miŋ 'gan: no
Ma	**fra**	**voi,**	**se**	**non**	**m'inganno,**
but	*among*	*you*	*if*	*not*	*myself I deceive*

'ɔd: dʒi	a 'lwɔ go	al 'ku na	'fɛ sta
oggi	**ha luogo**	**alcuna**	**festa?**
today	*takes place*	*some*	*celebration*

e	la	'spɔ za	ɛ	'kwel: la
E	**la**	**sposa?**	**è**	**quella?**
and	*the*	*bride*	*it is*	*that one*

ɛ	dʒen 'til	led: 'dʒa dra	'mol to
È	**gentil,**	**leggiadra**	**molto.**
she is	*refined*	*charming*	*much*

'ki o	ti	'mi ɾi
Ch'io	**ti**	**miri!**
that I	*you*	*[I] may gaze at*

o	il	'va go	'vol to
Oh!	**il**	**vago**	**volto!**
oh	*the*	*lovely*	*face*

tu non 'sa i   kon 'kwe i 'bɛʎː ʎi 'ɔkː ki
Tu non sai con quei begli occhi
you not you know with those beautiful eyes

'ko me 'dol tʃe il kɔr mi 'tokː ki
come dolce il cor mi tocchi,
how sweet the heart to me you touch

kwal ri 'kja mi 'a i pen 'sjɛr 'mjɛ i
qual richiami ai pensier miei
what you recall to the thoughts mine

a do 'ɾa bi le bel 'ta
adorabile beltà.
adorable beauty

'ɛ ɾa 'desː sa a kwal tu 'sɛ i
Era dessa, ah qual tu sei,
was she ah such as you [you] are

sul matː 'ti no delː le 'ta si
sul mattino dell'età, sì!
upon the morning of the age yes

I VESPRI SICILIANI (LES VÊPRES SICILIENNES)

music: Giuseppe Verdi

libretto: Eugène Scribe and Charles Duveyrier (after their libretto for Donizetti's opera *Le Duc d'Albe,* which was based on history)

note: The Italian translation by Fusinato and Caimi has become standard.

O tu, Palermo

o 'pa trja o 'ka ɾa 'pa trja
O patria, o cara patria,
oh homeland oh dear homeland

al 'fin ti 'vegː go
alfin ti veggo!
at last you I see

'lɛ zu le ti sa 'lu ta
L'esule ti saluta
the exile you greets

'do po si 'luŋ ga asː 'sɛn tsa
dopo sì lunga assenza.
after so long absence

il fjo 'ɾɛn te 'tu o 'swɔ lo
Il fiorente tuo suolo
the flowering your soil

ri 'pjɛn da 'mo ɾe 'i o 'ba tʃo
ripien d'amore io bacio,
full of love I [I] kiss

'rɛ ko il 'mi o 'vo to a te
reco il mio voto a te
I bring the my vow to you

kol 'bratː tʃo e il 'kɔ ɾe
col braccio e il core!
with the arm and the heart

o   tu   pa ˈlɛr mo   ˈtɛr: ra   a do ˈra ta
O   tu,   Palermo,   terra   adorata,
oh   you   Palermo   ground   adored

a   me   si   ˈka ɾo   ˈri zo   da ˈmor   a
a   me   sì   caro   riso   d'amor,   ah!
to   me   such   dear   smile   of love   ah

ˈal tsa   la   ˈfron te   ˈtan to   ol trad: ˈdʒa ta
alza   la   fronte   tanto   oltraggiata,
raise   the   brow   so much   desecrated

il   tu o   ri ˈpiʎ: ʎa   pri ˈmjɛr   splen ˈdor
il   tuo   ripiglia   primier   splendor!
the   your   take back again   former   splendor

ˈkjɛ zi   a ˈi ta   a   stra ˈnjɛ ɾe   nat: ˈtsjo ni
Chiesi   aita   a   straniere   nazioni,
I asked for   help   to   foreign   nations

ra miŋ ˈga i   per   ka ˈstɛl: la   e   tʃit: ˈta
ramingai   per   castella   e   città;
I roamed   through   castle   and   city

ma   in sen ˈsi bil   al   ˈfɛr vi do   ˈspro ne
ma   insensibil   al   fervido   sprone
but   indifferent   to the   fervid   incentive

di ˈtʃe a   tʃa ˈskun
dicea   ciascun:
said   each one

si tʃi ˈlja ni   o ˈvɛ   il   ˈpri sko   va ˈlor
Siciliani,   ov'è   il   prisco   valor?
Sicilians   where is   the   ancient   valor

su   sor ˈdʒe te   a   vit: ˈtɔ ɾja   al: lo ˈnor
Su,   sorgete   a   vittoria,   all'onor!
come on   rise   to   victory   to the honor

a   ˈtor na   al   pri ˈmje ɾo   ˈal mo   splen ˈdor
Ah,   torna   al   primiero   almo   splendor!
ah   return   to the   former   noble   splendor

ABOUT THE FRENCH IPA TRANSLITERATIONS
by Martha Gerhart

Following is a table of pronunciation for French lyric diction in singing as transliterated in this volume.

THE VOWELS

symbol	nearest equivalent in English	descriptive notes
[ɑ]	as in "father"	the "dark 'a'"
[a]	in English only in dialect; comparable to the Italian "a"	the "bright 'a'"
[e]	no equivalent in English; as in the German "Schnee"	the "closed 'e'": [i] in the [ɛ] position
[ɛ]	as in "bet"	the "open 'e'"
[i]	as in "feet"	
[o]	no equivalent in English as a pure vowel; approximately as in "open"	the "closed 'o'"
[ɔ]	as in "ought"	the "open 'o'"
[u]	as in "blue"	
[y]	no equivalent in English	[i] sustained with the lips rounded to a [u] position
[ø]	no equivalent in English	[e] sustained with the lips rounded almost to [u]
[œ] *	as in "earth" without pronouncing any "r"	[ɛ] with lips in the [ɔ] position
[ã]	no equivalent in English	the nasal "a": [ɔ] with nasal resonance added
[ɔ̃]	no equivalent in English	the nasal "o": [o] with nasal resonance added
[ɛ̃]	no equivalent in English	the nasal "e": as in English "cat" with nasal resonance added
[œ̃]	no equivalent in English	the nasal "œ": as in English "uh, huh" with nasal resonance added

* Some diction manuals transliterate the neutral, unstressed syllables in French as a "schwa" [ə].
Refer to authoritative published sources concerning such sophistications of French lyric diction.

THE SEMI-CONSONANTS

[ɥ]	no equivalent in English	a [y] in the tongue position of [i] and the lip position of [u]
[j]	as in "ewe," "yes"	a "glide"
[w]	as in "we," "want"	

THE CONSONANTS

[b]	as in "bad"	with a few exceptions
[c]	[k], as in "cart"	with some exceptions
[ç]	as in "sun"	when initial or medial, before *a*, *o*, or *u*
[d]	usually, as in "door"	becomes [t] in liaison
[f]	usually, as in "foot"	becomes [v] in liaison
[g]	usually, as in "gate"	becomes [k] in liaison; see also [ʒ]
[k]	as in "kite"	
[l]	as in "lift"	with some exceptions
[m]	as in "mint"	with a few exceptions
[n]	as in "nose"	with a few exceptions
[ɲ]	as in "onion"	almost always the pronunciation of the "gn" combination
[p]	as in "pass"	except when silent (final) and in a few rare words
[r] *	no equivalent in English	flipped (or occasionally rolled) "r"
[s]	as in "solo"	with exceptions; becomes [z] in liaison
[t]	as in "tooth"	with some exceptions
[v]	as in "voice"	
[x]	[ks] as in "extra," [gz] as in "exist," [z] as in "Oz," or [s] as in "sent"	becomes [z] in liaison
[z]	as in "zone"	with some exceptions
[ʒ]	as in "rouge"	usually, "g" when initial or mediant before *e*, *i*, or *y*; also, "j" in any position
[ʃ]	as in "shoe"	

* The conversational "uvular 'r'" is used in popular French song and cabaret but is not considered appropriate for singing in the classical repertoire.

LIAISON AND ELISION

Liaison is common in French. It is the sounding (linking) of a normally silent final consonant with the vowel (or mute h) beginning the next word. Its use follows certain rules; apart from the rules, the final choice as to whether or not to make a liaison depends on good taste and/or the advice of experts.

Examples of liaison, with their IPA:

les oiseaux   est ici
lɛ‿ zwa zo   ɛ‿ ti si

Elision is the linking of a consonant followed by a final unstressed *e* with the vowel (or mute *h*) beginning the next word.

examples, with their IPA: elle est   votre âme
ɛ‿ lɛ   vɔ‿ trɑ mœ

The linking symbol [‿] is given in these transliterations for both **elision** and for (recommended) **liaisons**.

FAUST

music: Charles Gounod
libretto: Jules Barbier and Michel Carré (after the drama by Johann Wolfgang von Goethe)

Le veau d'or

lœ	vo	dɔ‿	rɛ	tu ʒur	dœ bu
Le	**veau**	**d'or**	**est**	**toujours**	**debout!**
the	*calf*	*of gold*	*is*	*always*	*standing*

ɔ̃‿	nã sã sœ		sa	pɥi sã sœ	
On	**encense**		**sa**	**puissance**	
one	*burns incense to*		*its*	*power*	

dœ̃	bu	dy	mɔ̃‿	da	lo trœ	bu
d'un	**bout**	**du**	**monde**	**à**	**l'autre**	**bout!**
from one	*end*	*of the*	*world*	*to*	*the other*	*end*

pur	fɛ te	lɛ̃ fa‿	mi dɔ lœ	
Pour	**fêter**	**l'infâme**	**idole,**	
for	*to celebrate*	*the infamous*	*idol*	

rwa‿	ze	pœ plœ	kɔ̃ fɔ̃ dy	
rois	**et**	**peuples**	**confondu,**	
kings	*and*	*peoples*	*mingles*	

o	brɥi	sɔ̃ brœ	dɛ‿	ze ky
au	**bruit**	**sombre**	**des**	**écus,**
at the	*sound*	*sombre*	*of the*	*coins*

dã sœ‿	ty nœ	rɔ̃ dœ	fɔ lœ	
dansent	**une**	**ronde**	**folle,**	
dance	*a*	*circle*	*mad*	

o tur dœ	sɔ̃	pje dɛ stal	
autour de	**son**	**piédestal!**	
around	*its*	*pedestal*	

e	sa tã	kɔ̃ dɥi	lœ	bal
Et	**Satan**	**conduit**	**le**	**bal!**
and	*Satan*	*leads*	*the*	*dance*

lœ	vo	dɔ‿	rɛ	vɛ̃ kœr	de	djø
Le	**veau**	**d'or**	**est**	**vainqueur**	**des**	**dieux!**
the	*calf*	*of gold*	*is*	*vanquisher*	*of the*	*gods*

dã	sa	glwa rœ	de ri zwa rœ	
Dans	**sa**	**gloire**	**dérisoire**	
in	*his*	*glory*	*paltry*	

lœ	mɔ̃‿	trab ʒɛk‿	tɛ̃ syl‿	to	sjø
le	**monstre**	**abject**	**insulte**	**aux**	**cieux!**
the	*monster*	*despicable*	*is insulting*	*to the*	*heavens*

il	kɔ̃ tã‿	plo ra‿	ʒe trã ʒœ	a	sɛ
Il	**contemple,**	**ô**	**rage**	**étrange!**	**à**	**ses**
he	*contemplates*	*oh*	*frenzy*	*terrible*	*at*	*his*

pje	lœ	ʒã‿	ry mɛ̃	
pieds	**le**	**genre**	**humain,**	
feet	*the*	*race*	*human*	

sœ ry ã‿	lœ	fɛ‿	rã	mɛ̃
se ruant,	**le**	**fer**	**en**	**main,**
throwing itself	*the*	*sword*	*in*	*hand*

34

dã   lœ   sã   e   dã   la   fã ʒœ
dans   le   sang   et   dans   la   fange,
into   the   blood   and   into   the   filth

u   bri jœ   lar dã   me tal
où   brille   l'ardent   métal!
where   shines   the blazing   metal

e   sa tã   kɔ̃ dyi   lœ   bal
Et   Satan   conduit   le   bal!
and   Satan   leads   the   dance

Vous qui faites l'endormie

vu   ki   fɛ tœ lã dɔr mi œ
Vous   qui   faites l'endormie,
you   who   pretend to be asleep

nã tã de vu   pɑ
n'entendez-vous   pas,
not do hear you   [not]

o   ka tœ ri nœ   ma mi œ
ô   Catherine,   ma mie,
o   Catherine   my love

ma   vwa‿   ze   mɛ   pɑ
ma   voix   et   mes   pas?
my   voice   and   my   steps

ɛ̃ si   tɔ̃   ga lã   ta pɛ lœ
Ainsi   ton   galant   t'appelle,
thus   your   gallant   you calls

e   tɔ̃   kœr   lã krwɑ
et   ton   cœur   l'en croit.
and   your   heart   him trusts in

a   a   a   a
Ah!   ah!   ah!   ah!
ah   ah   ah   ah

nu vrœ   ta   pɔr tœ   ma   bɛ lœ
N'ouvre   ta   porte,   ma   belle,
not open   your   door   my   beautiful one

kœ   la   ba‿   go   dwa
que   la   bague   au   doigt!
[except with]   the   ring   on the   finger

ka tœ ri nœ   kœ   ʒa dɔ rœ
Catherine   que   j'adore,
Catherine   whom   I adore

pur kwa   rœ fy ze
pourquoi   refuser
why   to refuse

a   la mã   ki   vu‿   zɛ̃ plɔ rœ
à   l'amant   qui   vous   implore
to   the lover   who   you   implores

œ   si   du   bɛ ze
un   si   doux   baiser?
a   so   sweet   kiss

ẽ si tɔ̃ ga lã sy pli œ
Ainsi ton galant supplie,
thus your gallant beseeches

e tɔ̃ kœr lã krwɑ
et ton cœur l'en croit.
and your heart him trusts in

a a a a
Ah! ah! ah! ah!
ah ah ah ah

nœ dɔ‿ nœ̃ bɛ ze ma mi œ
Ne donne un baiser, ma mie,
not give a kiss my love

kœ la ba‿ go dwa
que la bague au doigt!
[except with] the ring on the finger

a a a a a a
Ah! ah! ah! ah! ah! ah!
ah ah ah ah ah ah

LES HUGUENOTS
music: Giacomo Meyerbeer
libretto: Eugène Scribe and Emile Deschamps (after history)

Pour les couvents c'est fini (Piff, paff)

vɔ lɔ̃ tje
Volontiers,
willingly

œ̃ vjɛ‿ jɛr y gœ no
un vieil air huguenot
an old air Huguenot

kɔ̃ trœ lɛ ʒã dy pa‿
contre les gens du pape
against the people of the pope

pe lœ sɛk sœ dɑ na blœ
et le sexe damnable;
and the sex damnable

vu lœ kɔ nɛ se bjɛ̃
vous le connaissez bien—
you it know well

sɛ nɔ‿ trɛr de kɔ̃ bɑ
c'est notre air des combats,
it is our song of the battles

sœ lɥi dœ la rɔ ʃɛ lœ
celui de la Rochelle:
that one from the Rochelle

se tɛ‿ ta lɔr
c'était alors
it was then

ko   brɥi   dɛ   tɑ̃ bur
qu'au   bruit   des   tambours,
that at the   sound   of the   drums

dɛ   sɛ̃ ba lœ
des   cymbales,
of the   cymbals

a kɔ̃ pa ɲe   dy   pif   paf   puf
accompagné   du   piff,   paff,   pouff
accompanied   by the   bang   bang   boom

dɛ   ba lœ
des   balles
of the   bullets

ʒœ   ʃɑ̃ tɛ
je   chantais:
I   sang

pif   paf
piff,   paff.
bang   bang

pur   lɛ   ku vɑ̃   sɛ   fi ni
Pour   les   couvents   c'est   fini,
for   the   convents   it is   finished

lɛ   mwa nœ   a   tɛ rœ
les   moines   à   terre;
the   monks   at   ground

gɛ‿   ra   tu   ka go   be ni
guerre   à   tout   cagot   béni,
war   to   every   hypocrite   blessed

pa pi stœ   la   gɛ rœ
papistes   la   guerre.
papists   the   war

li vrɔ̃‿   za   la   flɑ‿   mo   fɛr
Livrons   à   la   flamme   aux   fers
let us deliver   to   the   flame   at the   sword

lœr   tɑ̃ plœ   dɑ̃ fɛr
leurs   temples   d'enfer;
their   temples   of hell

tɛ ra sɔ̃ lɛ   sɛr nɔ̃ lɛ
terrassons-les,   cernons-les,
let's knock down them   beseige them

fra pɔ̃ lɛ   pɛr sɔ̃ lɛ
frappons-les,   perçons-les,
strike them   run them through

pif   paf   puf
piff,   paff,   pouff.
bang   bang   boom

kil   plœ rœ
Qu'ils   pleurent,
that they   weep

kil plœ rœ
Qu'ils pleurent,
that they weep

kil mœ rœ
qu'ils meurent,
that they die

mɛ grɑ sœ ʒa mɛ
mais grâce jamais,
but pardon never

nɔ ʒa mɛ
non, jamais.
no never

ʒa mɛ mɔ̃ bra nœ trɑ̃ bla
Jamais mon bras ne trembla
never my arm [not] will tremble

o plɛ̃ tœ dɛ fa mœ
aux plaintes des femmes.
at the moans of the women

ma lœ‿ ra sɛ da li la
Malheur à ces Dalilas
woe to those Dalilas

ki pɛr dœ le‿ za mœ
qui perdent les âmes;
who lose their souls

bri zɔ̃ o trɑ̃ ʃɑ̃ dy fɛr
brisons au tranchant du fer
let's break at the cutting of the sword

lœr ʃar mœ dɑ̃ fɛr
leurs charmes d'enfer.
their charms of hell

sɛ bo de mɔ̃ ʃa se lɛ
Ces beaux démons, chassez-les,
those beautiful demons chase them

tra ke lɛ fra pe lɛ
traquez-les, frappez-les,
round up them strike them

pif paf puf
piff, paff, pouff.
bang bang boom

LA JOLIE FILLE DE PERTH

music: Georges Bizet
libretto: J.H. Vernoy de St. Georges and Jules Adenis (after the novel by Sir Walter Scott)

Quand la flamme de l'amour

la la la   tra la la   tra la
La la la!...   tra la la!...   tra la!
la la la   tra la la   tra la

kɑ̃   la   flɑ mœ   dœ   la mur
Quand   la   flamme   de   l'amour
when   the   flame   of   the love

bry lœ   lɑ mœ   nɥi̯   te   ʒur
brûle   l'âme   nuit   et   jour,
burns   the soul   night   and   day

pur   le tɛ̃ drœ   kɛl kœ fwa
pour   l'éteindre   quelquefois,
for   it to extinguish   sometimes

sɑ̃   mœ plɛ̃ drœ   mwa   ʒœ   bwa
sans   me plaindre,   moi   je   bois!
without   complaining   me   I   drink

ʒœ   ri   ʒœ   ʃɑ̃ tœ
Je   ris!   Je   chante!
I   laugh   I   sing

ʒœ   ri   ʒœ   ʃɑ̯̃   te   ʒœ   bwa
Je   ris,   je   chante   et   je   bois!
I   laugh   I   sing   and   I   drink

tra   la   la   la   la   a   tra   la   la
Tra   la   la   la   la!   Ah!   tra   la   la!...
tra   la   la   la   la   ah   tra   la   la

si̯ lɛ̯   ty nœ   tri stœ   fɔ li œ
S'il est   une   triste   folie,
if there is   a   sad   folly

sɛ   sɛ lœ   dœ̃   po̯   vra mu rø
c'est   celle   d'un   pauvre   amoureux
it is   that   of a   poor   lover

kœ̃   rœ gar   dœ   fa̯   my mi li
qu'un   regard   de   femme   humilie,
whom a   look   from   woman   humbles

kœ̃   mo   pø   rɑ̃ drœ   ma lœ rø
qu'un   mot   peut   rendre   malheureux,
whom a   word   is able   to make   unhappy

e lɑs
hélas!
alas

kɑ̯̃   tɔ̯̃   nɛ mœ   sɑ̯̃   zɛ spwar
Quand   on   aime   sans   espoir,
when   one   loves   without   hope

lœ   sjɛl   mɛ mœ   dœ vjɛ̃   nwar
le   ciel   même   devient   noir.
the   heaven   even   becomes   dark

39

e	lo tɛ sœ	mɔ̃	fla kɔ̃
Eh!	**l'hôtesse...**	**mon**	**flacon!**
hey	*the hostess*	*my*	*bottle*

kœ	ʒi	lɛ sœ	ma	rɛ zɔ̃
que	**j'y**	**laisse**	**ma**	**raison!**
that	*I there*	*may leave*	*my*	*reason*

tra	la	la	la	la
Tra	**la**	**la**	**la**	**la!...**
tra	*la*	*la*	*la*	*la*

MANON
music: Jules Massenet
libretto: Henri Meilhac and Philippe Gille (after the novel *L'Histoire du Chevalier des Grieux et de Manon Lescaut* by Abbé Prévost)

Épouse quelque brave fille

lɛ	grã	mo	kœ	vwa la
Les	**grands**	**mots**	**que**	**voilà!**
the	*lofty*	*words*	*that*	*there is*

kɛ lœ	ru	ta ty	dɔ̃	sɥi vi œ
Quelle	**route**	**as-tu**	**donc**	**suivie,**
what	*path*	*have you*	*then*	*followed*

e	kœ	sɛ ty	dœ	sɛ tœ	vi œ
et	**que**	**sais-tu**	**de**	**cette**	**vie**
and	*what*	*know you*	*of*	*this*	*life*

pur	pã se	kɛ lœ	fi ni	la
pour	**penser**	**qu'elle**	**finit**	**là?**
in order	*to think*	*that it*	*ends*	*there*

e pu zœ	kɛl kœ	bra vœ	fi jœ
Épouse	**quelque**	**brave**	**fille**
marry	*some*	*fine*	*girl*

di ɲœ	dœ	nu	di ɲœ	dœ	twa
digne	**de**	**nous,**	**digne**	**de**	**toi;**
worthy	*of*	*us*	*worthy*	*of*	*you*

dœ vjɛ̃	zœ̃	pɛ rœ	dœ	fa mi jœ
deviens	**un**	**père**	**de**	**famille**
become	*a*	*father*	*of*	*family*

ni	pi rœ	ni	mɛ jœr	kœ	mwa
ni	**pire,**	**ni**	**meilleur**	**que**	**moi:**
neither	*worse*	*nor*	*better*	*than*	*me*

lœ	sjɛl	nã	vø	pɑ	da vã ta ʒœ
le	**ciel**	**n'en**	**veut**	**pas**	**davantage.**
the	*heaven*	*not of it*	*wishes*	*[not]*	*more*

sɛ	la	lœ	dœ vwar
C'est	**là**	**le**	**devoir,**
it is	*there*	*the*	*duty*

ã tã ty
entends-tu?
understand you

sɛ   la   lœ   dœ vwar
C'est   là   le   devoir!
it is   there   the   duty

la   vɛr ty   ki   fɛ   dy   ta pa ʒœ
La   vertu   qui   fait   du   tapage
the   virtue   which   makes   of the   uproar

nɛ   de ʒa   ply   dœ   la   vɛr ty
n'est   déjà   plus   de   la   vertu!
not is   at all   more   of   the   virtue

ABOUT THE GERMAN IPA TRANSLITERATIONS
by Irene Spiegelman

TRANSLATIONS

As every singer has experienced, word-by-word translations are usually awkward, often not understandable, especially in German where the verb usually is split up with one part in second position of the main clause and the rest at the end of the sentence. Sometimes it is a second verb, sometimes it is a little word that looks like a preposition. Since prepositions never come by themselves, these are usually *separable prefixes to the verb*. In order to look up the meaning of the verb this prefix has to be reunited with the verb in order to find the correct meaning in the dictionary. They cannot be looked up by themselves. Therefore, in the word-by-word translation they are marked with [1]) and do not show any words.

Note: In verbs with separable prefixes, the prefix gets the emphasis. If a separable prefix appears at the end of the sentence, it still needs to be stressed and since many of them start with vowels they even might be glottaled for emphasis.

Also, there are many *reflexive verbs* in German that are not reflexive in English, also the reflexive version of a verb in German often means something very different than the meaning found if the verb is looked up by itself. Reflexive pronouns that are grammatically necessary but do not have a meaning by themselves do not show a translation underneath. They are marked with [2]).

Another difference in the use of English and German is that German is using the Present Perfect Tense of the verb where English prefers the use of the Simple Past of the verb. In cases like that, the translation appears under the conjugated part of the verb and none underneath the past participle of the verb at the end of the sentence. Those cases are marked with [3]).

One last note concerning the translations: English uses possessive pronouns much more often then German does. So der/die/das in German have at appropriate points been translated as my/your/his.

PRONUNCIATION (EXTENDED IPA SYMBOLS)

The IPA symbols that have been used for the German arias are basically those used in Langenscheidt dictionaries. Other publications have refined some symbols, but after working with young singers for a long time, I find that they usually don't remember which is which sign when the ones for long closed vowels (a and ɑ, or ʏ and y) are too close, and especially with the signs for the open and closed u-umlauts they usually cannot tell which they handwrote into their scores. To make sure that a vowel should be closed there is ":" behind the symbol, i.e. [by:p laɪn]

After having been encouraged to sing on a vowel as long as possible, often the consonants are cut too short. The rule is, **"Vowels can be used to make your voice shine, consonants will help your interpretation!"** This is very often is totally neglected in favor of long vowels, even when the vowels are supposed to be short. Therefore, double consonants show up here in the IPA line. This suggests that they should at least not be neglected. There are voiced consonants on which it is easy to sing (l, m, n) and often give the text an additional dimension. That is not true for explosive consonants (d, t, k), but they open the vowels right in front of them. So the double consonants in these words serve here as reminders. German does not require to double the consonants the way Italian does, but that Italian technique might help to move more quickly to the consonant, and therefore open the vowel or at least don't stretch it, which sometimes turns it into a word with a different meaning altogether.

One idea that is heard over and over again is: "There is no legato in German." The suggestions that are marked here with ⇨ in the IPA line show that **that is not true.** Always elided can be words ending in a vowel with the next word beginning with a vowel. Words that end with a -t sound can be combined with the next word that starts with a t- or a d-. A word ending in -n can be connected to the following beginning -n. But words ending in consonants can also be elided with the next word starting with a vowel. (example: Dann [dan⇨n] könnt' [kœn⇨n⇨] ich [⇨tɪç] mit [mɪt] Fürsten ['fʏr stən] mich ['mɛs⇨sən]). In this example, the arrow symbol suggests to use the double consonant, but also that the end-t in "könnt'" could be used at the beginning of "ich" which makes the word "ich" much less important (which it usually is in German), and could help to shape the words "Fürsten" und "messen" with more importance.

Within the IPA line, sometimes the "⇨" symbol is only at the end of a word and means that combining this word with the next is absolutely possible if it helps the interpretation of the text or the singer does not want to interrupt the beauty of the musical line. The same fact is true if the "⇨" symbol appears within a word and suggests combining syllables. (Since English syllables are viewed differently than German syllables, the IPA line is broken down into German syllables with suggestions for vocal combinations.) The only consonant that should not be combined with the next word is "r," because there are too many combinations that form new words (example: der Eine, the one and only, should not become [de: raɪ nə], the pure one).

One last remark about pronunciation that seems to have become an issue in the last few years: How does one pronounce the a-umlaut = ä. Some singers have been told in their diction classes that ä is pronounced like a closed e. That may be the case in casual language and can be heard on German television. But when the texts that we are dealing with were written the sound was either a long or short open e sound ['mɛ: tçən, ʃpɛːt, 'hɛl tə].

Considering the language, how does one make one's voice shine and still use the text for a sensible interpretation? Look for the words within a phrase that are important to you as the interpreter, as the person who believes what he/she is conveying. In those words use the consonants as extensively as possible. [zzze: llə] and [llli: bə] are usually more expressive than [ze: lə] and [li: bə] , also glottal the beginning vowels. Use the surrounding words for singing legato and show off the voice.

The IPA line not only shows correct pronunciation but is also giving guidelines for interpretation. For instance, R's may be rolled or flipped, or words may be connected or separated at any time as long as they help you with your feeling for the drama of the text. But you are the person who has to decide! Be discriminating! Know what you want to say! Your language will fit with the music perfectly.

THE "R" IN GERMAN DICTION

When most Germans speak an "r" in front of a vowel, it is a sound produced between the far back of the tongue and the uvula, almost like a gargling sound. The r's at the end of syllables take on different sounds and often have a vowel-like quality.

In classical singing, the practice is to use "Italian r's". Since trilling the r at the tip of the tongue seems to be easy for most singers, many texts are rendered with any overdone r's, which are remotely possible. As a result, the r's take over the whole text and diminish the meaning and phrasing of the sentences. By being discriminating in using rolled r's in an opera text, the phrasing, i.e. interpretation, as well as the chance of understanding the sung text can be improved.

Essentially, there are three categories of words with different suggestions about the use of r's:

ALWAYS ROLL THE R	END-R'S IN SHORT ONE-SYLLABLE WORDS	END-R'S IN PREFIXES AND SUFFIXES
a) before vowels: **R**ose ['ro: zə] t**r**agen ['tra: gən] sp**r**echen ['ʃprɛ: xən] T**r**ug [tru:k] füh**r**en ['fy: rən] b) after vowels in the main syllable of the word: be**r**gen ['bɛr gən] He**r**z [hɛrts] Schwe**r**t [ʃve:rt] du**r**ch [dʊrç] gewo**r**ben [gə 'vɔr bən] ha**r**t [hart]	End-r's in short one-syllable words that have a closed vowel can be replaced with a short a-vowel, marked in the IPA line with ᵃ. der [de:ᵃ] er [e:ᵃ] wir [vi:ᵃ] hier [hi:ᵃ] vor [fo:ᵃ] nur [nu:ᵃ] **Note:** **After an a-vowel a replacement of r by ᵃ would not sound. Therefore end-r's after any a should be rolled.** **war [va:r]** **gar [ga:r]**	Prefixes: ver- er- zer- Here, e and r could be pronounced as a schwa-sound, almost like a short open e combined with a very short ᵃ. If desired, the r could also be flipped with one little flip in order not to overpower the main part of the word which is coming up. In the IPA-line this is marked with ʀ. verbergen [fɛʀ 'bɛr gən] erklären [ɛʀ 'klɛ: rən] Suffix: -er These suffixes are most of the time not important for the interpretation of the text. Therefore, the schwa-sound as explained above works in most cases very well. It is marked in the IPA-line with ɚ. e-Suffixes are marked with ə. guter ['gu: tɚ] gute ['gu: tə] Winter ['vɪn tɚ] Meistersinger ['maɪ stɚ sɪ ŋɚ] (compound noun, both parts end in -er)

DIE ENTFÜHRUNG AUS DEM SERAIL
music: Wolfgang Amadeus Mozart
libretto: Gottlieb Stephanie the younger (after a libretto by Christoph Friedrich Bretzner)

O, wie will ich triumphiren

o: vi: vɪll⇨   ɪç   tri: ʊm ˈfi: rən
O,   wie   will   ich   triumphieren,
Oh,   how   shall   I   exalt,

vɛnn   zi: oyç   tsʊm   ˈrɪçt plats   ˈfy: rən
wenn   sie   euch   zum   Richtplatz   führen,
when   they   you   to the   gallows   lead,

ʊnt⇨   di: ˈhɛːl zə   ˈʃny: rən   tsu:
und   die   Hälse   schnüren   zu.
and   your   necks   tie   tightly.

ˈhʏp fən   vɪll⇨   ɪç   ˈla xən   ˈʃprɪ ŋən
Hüpfen   will   ich,   lachen,   springen,
Skip   will   I,   laugh,   jump,

ʊnt   aɪn   ˈfrɔy dən ˈli:⇨tçən   ˈzɪ ŋən
und   ein   Freudenliedchen   singen;
and   a   joyful song   sing;,

dɛnn   nu:n   ha:⇨   ⇨bɪç   fo:ᵃ   ɔyç   ru:
denn   nun   hab'   ich   vor   euch   Ruh'.
for   now   have   I   from   you   peace.

ʃlaɪçt   nu:ᵃ   ˈzɔy bɚ lɪç⇨   ʊnt   ˈlaɪ zə
Schleicht   nur   säuberlich   und   leise,
Sneak   only   carefully   and   carefully,

i:ᵃ   fɛʁ ˈdamm tən   ˈha: rɛms ˈmɔy zə
ihr   verdammten   Harems-mäuse,
you   damned   harem's mice,

ʊn zɚ   o:ᵃ   ɛnt⇨ ˈdɛkt   ɔyç   ʃo:n
unser   Ohr   entdeckt   euch   schon;
our   ear   will discover   you   definitely;

ʊnt   e: i:ᵃ   ʊns   kœnnt   ɛnt ˈʃprɪ ŋən
und   eh'   ihr   uns   könnt   entspringen,
and   before   you   from us   can   escape,

ze:t⇨   i:ᵃ   ɔyç⇨   ɪn   ˈʊn zɚn   ˈʃlɪ ŋən
seht   ihr   euch   in   unsern   Schlingen,
will find   you   yourselves   in   our   traps,

ʊnt   ɛʁ ˈha ʃət   ˈɔy rən   lo:n
und   erhaschet   euren   Lohn.
and   will catch   your   reward.

DER FREISCHÜTZ
music: Carl Maria von Weber
libretto: Johann Friedrich Kind (after a story by Johann August Apel and Friedrich Laun and Gothic legend)

Schweig'! schweig'! damit dich niemand warnt

ʃvaɪk
Schweig'!
Keep quiet!

da 'mɪt⇨	dɪç	'niː mant	varnt
damit	**dich**	**niemand**	**warnt.**
so that	*you*	*nobody*	*(can) warn.*

'ʃvaɪ ɡə
Schweige!
Keep quiet!

deːᵃ	hœl⇨ lə	nɛts
Der	**Hölle**	**Netz**
(The)	*hell's*	*net*

hat⇨	dɪç	ʊm 'ɡarnt
hat	**dich**	**umgarnt!**
has	*you*	*ensnared!*

nɪçts	kan⇨n	fɔm	tiː fən	fal⇨l
Nichts	**kann**	**vom**	**tiefen**	**Fall**
Nothing	*can*	*from the*	*deep*	*fall*

dɪç	'rɛt⇨ tən
dich	**retten!**
you	*save!*

ʊm 'ɡeːpt⇨	iːn	iːᵃ	'ɡaɪ stɚ
Umgebt	**ihn,**	**ihr**	**Geister**
Surround	*him,*	*you*	*spirits*

mɪt⇨	'dʊŋ kəl	bə 'ʃvɪŋt
mit	**Dunkel**	**beschwingt;**
with	*darkness*	*enlivened;*

ʃoːn	trɛːkt	eːᵃ	'knɪr ʃənt
schon	**trägt**	**er**	**knirschend**
already	*bears*	*he*	*grudgingly*

'ɔy rə	'kɛt⇨ tən
eure	**Ketten!**
your	*chains!*

triː 'ʊmf
Triumph!
Victory!

diː	'ra xə	ɡə 'lɪŋt
Die	**Rache**	**gelingt!**
(The)	*revenge*	*succeeds!*

DIE LUSTIGEN WEIBER VON WINDSOR

music: Otto Nicolai

libretto: Hermann von Mosenthal (after the comedy by William Shakespeare)

Als Büblein klein

als	'byː⇨ plaɪn	'klaɪn	an	deːᵃ	'mʊt⇨ tɚ	brʊst
Als	**Büblein**	**klein**	**an**	**der**	**Mutter**	**Brust,**
When	*a little boy,*	*tiny,*	*at*	*my*	*mother's*	*breast,*

hɔp	'haɪs⇨ sa	baɪ	'reː gən⇨	ʊnt⇨	'vɪnt
hopp	**heißa**	**bei**	**Regen**	**und**	**Wind,**
very	*happy*	*in*	*rain*	*and*	*wind,*

daː	vaːr	deːᵃ	'zɛk⇨	⇨tʃoːn	'maɪ nə	'lʊst
da	**war**	**der**	**Sekt**	**schon**	**meine**	**Lust,**
then	*was*	*the*	*sparkling wine*	*already*	*my*	*pleasure,*

dɛn	deːᵃ	're: gən	deːᵃ	'reː⇨ gnət	'jeː⇨ klɪçən	'taːk
denn	**der**	**Regen,**	**der**	**regnet**	**jeglichen**	**Tag!**
for	*the*	*rain,*	*it*	*rains*	*every*	*day!*

kɔm	'braʊ nə	'han⇨nə	heːᵃ
Komm,	**braune**	**Hanne,**	**her,**
Come,	*sun tanned*	*Jane,*	*here,*

'raɪç	miːᵃ	diː	'kan⇨ nə	'heːᵃ
reich	**mir**	**die**	**Kanne**	**her,**
pass	*me*	*the*	*jug*	*¹)*

'fʏl	miːᵃ	deːn	'ʃlaʊx
füll'	**mir**	**den**	**Schlauch!**
fill	*for me*	*the*	*wine skin!*

'lœʃ	miːᵃ	deːᵃ	'keː lə	'brant
Lösch'	**mir**	**der**	**Kehle**	**Brand.**
Quench	*me*	*my*	*throat's*	*fire.*

'trɪŋ kən	ɪst	kaɪ nə	ʃant
Trinken	**ist**	**keine**	**Schand';**
Drinking	*is*	*no*	*disgrace;*

'ba xʊs	'traŋk	'aʊx	jaː
Bacchus	**trank**	**auch,**	**ja!**
Bacchus	*drank*	*too,*	*really!*

nuːn	ɪn	'poː ziː tuːᵃ
Nun	**in**	**Positur!**
Now	*into*	*position!*

'hal tət	ɔyç	bə 'raɪt
Haltet	**euch**	**bereit!**
Keep	*yourselves*	*ready!*

maxt⇨	diː	'keː lən	'vaɪt
Macht	**die**	**Kehlen**	**weit!**
Open	*your*	*throats*	*widely!*

aɪns	tsvaɪ	ʊnt⇨	draɪ
Eins,	**zwei**	**und**	**drei.**
One,	*two*	*and*	*three.*

ʊnt	als⇨	ɪç	fɛʀ 'treː tən	diː	'kɪn dɚ ʃuː
Und	**als**	**ich**	**vertreten**	**die**	**Kinderschuh',**
And	*when*	*I*	*outgrew*	*my*	*childhood shoes,*

hɔp	haɪs⇨sa	baɪ	'reː gən⇨	ʊnt	vɪnt
hopp	**heißa**	**bei**	**Regen**	**und**	**Wind,**
very	*happy*	*during*	*rain*	*and*	*wind.*

da	'ʃlɔs⇨ sən	diː	'mɛː dəl	zɪç	voːᵃ miːᵃ	tsuː
da	**schlossen**	**die**	**Mädel**	**sich**	**vor mir**	**zu,**
then	*locked*	*the*	*girls*	*themselves*	*from me*	*in,*

dɛn	deːᵃ	'reː gən	deːᵃ	'reː⇨ gnət	'jeː⇨ klɪçən	'taːk
denn	**der**	**Regen,**	**der**	**regnet**	**jeglichen**	**Tag!**
for	*the*	*rain,*	*it*	*rains*	*every*	*day!*

ʊnt	ɪst⇨	diː	'ta ʃə	'leːᵃ
Und	**ist**	**die**	**Tasche**	**leer,**
And	*is*	*the*	*pocket*	*empty,*

ʊnt	vɪrt⇨	diː	'fla ʃə	'leːᵃ
und	**wird**	**die**	**Flasche**	**leer,**
and	*becomes*	*the*	*bottle*	*empty,*

kɔmt	'vʏr fəl	raʊs
kommt	**Würfel**	**raus!**
(then) come	*dice*	*out!*

'glʏk	ɪst⇨	aɪn	'ʃprøː dɚ	'gast
Glück	**ist**	**ein**	**spröder**	**Gast;**
Good fortune	*is*	*a*	*stubborn*	*guest;*

veːᵃ	ɛs	baɪm	ʃɔ⇨ pfə	fast
wer	**es**	**beim**	**Schopfe**	**fasst,**
the one	*it*	*by the*	*hair*	*grabs,*

'fyːrt⇨	ɛs	nax⇨	'haʊs	jaː
führt	**es**	**nach**	**Haus,**	**ja!**
will lead	*it*	[4])	*home,*	*yes!*

¹) Separable prefix to the verb "herreichen" (pass)

⁴) Idiomatic phrase: "nach Haus" (home), therefore no translation for "nach"

48

DIE ZAUBERFLÖTE

music: Wolfgang Amadeus Mozart
libretto: Emanuel Schikaneder (loosely based on a fairy tale by Wieland)

O Isis und Osiris

o:	'iː zɪs	ʊnt	'oː ziː rɪs	'ʃɛŋ kət
O	**Isis**	**und**	**Osiris,**	**schenket**
Oh	*Isis*	*and*	*Osiris,*	*bestow*

deːᵃ	'vaɪs haɪt	ɡaɪst⇨	deːm	'nɔy ən	paːr
der	**Weisheit**	**Geist**	**dem**	**neuen**	**Paar!**
the	*wisdom's*	*spirit*	*upon the*	*new*	*couple!*

diː	iːᵃ	deːᵃ	'van drɚ	'ʃrɪt⇨ tə	'lɛŋ kət
Die	**ihr**	**der**	**Wandrer**	**Schritte**	**lenket,**
You	*who*	*the*	*travelers'*	*steps*	*lead,*

ʃtɛːrkt	mɪt	ɡə 'dʊlt	ziː	ɪn	ɡə 'faːr
stärkt	**mit**	**Geduld**	**sie**	**in**	**Gefahr.**
strengthen	*with*	*patience*	*them*	*in*	*danger.*

lasst⇨	ziː	deːᵃ	'pryː fʊŋ	'frʏç tə	'zeː (h)ən
Lasst	**sie**	**der**	**Prüfung**	**Früchte**	**sehen,**
Let	*them*	*(the)*	*trials'*	*results*	*recognize,*

dɔx	'zɔl⇨l tən	ziː	tsuː	'graː bə	'geː (h)ən
doch	**sollten**	**sie**	**zu**	**Grabe**	**gehen,**
but	*should*	*they*	*to their*	*grave*	*go,*

zoː	loːnt	deːᵃ	'tuː ɡənt	'kyː nən	laʊf
so	**lohnt**	**der**	**Tugend**	**kühnen**	**Lauf,**
then	*reward*	*(the)*	*virtue's*	*brave*	*course,*

neːm⇨	⇨tsiː	ɪn	'ɔy rən	'voːn zɪts	aʊf
nehmt	**sie**	**in**	**euren**	**Wohnsitz**	**auf.**
receive	*them*	*in*	*your*	*kingdom*	*¹)*

¹) Separable prefix to the verb "aufnehmen" (receive, welcome)

In diesen heil'gen Hallen

ɪn   di: zən   'haɪl gən   'hal⇨ lən
In   **diesen**   **heil'gen**   **Hallen**
In   *these*   *sacred*   *halls*

kɛnnt⇨   man   di: 'ra xə   nɪçt
kennt   **man**   **die**   **Rache**   **nicht,**
knows   *one*   *(the)*   *revenge*   *not,*

ʊnt   ɪst   aɪn   mɛnʃ   gə 'fal⇨ lən
und   **ist**   **ein**   **Mensch**   **gefallen,**
and   *did*   *a*   *human being*   *fall,*

fy:rt   'li: bə   i:n   tsu:ᵃ   pflɪçt
führt   **Liebe**   **ihn**   **zur**   **Pflicht.**
leads   *love*   *him*   *to his*   *duty.*

dan⇨n   'van dəlt   e:ᵃ   an   'frɔyn dəs   hant
Dann   **wandelt**   **er**   **an**   **Freundes**   **Hand**
Then   *travels*   *he*   *by a*   *friend's*   *hand*

fɛʀ 'gny:kt   ʊnt   fro: ɪns   'bɛs⇨s rə   lant
vergnügt   **und**   **froh**   **ins**   **bess're**   **Land.**
joyful   *and*   *happy*   *to a*   *better*   *land.*

ɪn   di: zən   'haɪl gən   'maʊ ɚn
In   **diesen**   **heil'gen**   **Mauern,**
In   *these*   *sacred*   *walls*

vo: mɛnʃ   de:n   'mɛn ʃən   li:pt
wo   **Mensch**   **den**   **Menschen**   **liebt,**
where   *man*   *the*   *fellow man*   *loves,*

kan⇨n   kaɪn   fɛʀ 'rɛ: tɚ   'laʊ ɚn
kann   **kein**   **Verräter**   **lauern,**
can   *no*   *traitor*   *hide,*

vaɪl   man   de:m   faɪnt   fɛʀ 'gi:pt
weil   **man**   **dem**   **Feind**   **vergibt.**
because   *one*   *the*   *enemy*   *forgives.*

ve:n   'zɔl çə   'le: rən   nɪçt   ɛʀ 'frɔyn
Wen   **solche**   **Lehren**   **nicht**   **erfreun,**
Whomever   *such*   *teachings*   *not*   *please*

fɛʀ 'di: nət   nɪçt   aɪn   mɛnʃ   tsu: zaɪn
verdienet   **nicht**   **ein**   **Mensch**   **zu**   **sein.**
deserves   *not*   *a*   *human being*   *to*   *be.*

THE INTERNATIONAL PHONETIC ALPHABET FOR ENGLISH

An overview of all the sounds found in American Standard (AS),
British Received (RP), and Mid-Atlantic (MA) Pronunciations.
by Kathryn LaBouff

CONSONANTS:

The following symbols are identical to the letters of our English (Roman) Alphabet:

[b], [d], [f], [g], [h], [k], [l], [m], [n], [p], [s], [t], [v], [w], [z]

The symbols below are NEW symbols added because no corresponding symbols exist in the Roman alphabet:

SYMBOL	KEY WORDS
[ŋ]	sing, think
[θ]	thin, thirst
[ð]	thine, this
[ʍ]	whisper, when
[j]	you, yes
[ʃ]	she, sure
[tʃ]	choose, church
[ʒ]	vision, azure
[dʒ]	George, joy
[ɹ]	red, remember, every (the burred r)
[ʀ]	righteousness, great, realm (rolled r)
[r]	very, far away, forever (flip r used between vowels)

VOWELS:

SYMBOL	KEY WORDS
[ɑ]	father, hot ("o" spellings in AS only)
[ɛ]	wed, many, bury
[ɪ]	hit, been, busy
[i]	me, chief, feat, receive
[ɨ]	pretty, lovely
[t]	cat, marry, ask**, charity
[u]	too, wound, blue, juice
[ju]	view, beautiful, usual, tune
[ɯ]	book, bosom, cushion, full
[o]	obey, desolate, melody (unstressed syllables only)
[ɒ]	on, not, honest, God (RP & MA only)*
[ɔ]	awful, call, daughter, sought (AS)
[ɔ̹]	awful, call, daughter, sought (RP & MA)
[ɜ˞]	learn, burn, rehearse, journey (AS)
[ɜʳ]	learn, burn, rehearse, journey (RP & MA)
[ɚ]	father, doctor, vulgar, elixir (AS)
[əʳ]	father, doctor, vulgar, elixir (RP & MA)
[ʌ]	hum, blood, trouble, judge (stressed syllables)
[ə]	sofa, heaven, nation, joyous (unstressed syllables)

*The use of rolled and flipped R's and the short open o vowel are used in the British RP British and Mid-Atlantic dialect. They should not be used in American Standard dialect.

**[ɜ˞ and [ɚ] are the r colored vowels characteristic of American Standard Pronunciation, AS.

[ɜʳ] and [əʳ] are the REDUCED r colored vowels found in British RP, and Mid-Atlantic, MA Pronunciations.

DIPHTHONGS:

SYMBOL	KEY WORDS
[aɪ]	night, buy, sky
[eɪ]	day, break, reign
[ɔɪ]	boy, voice, toil
[oʊ]	no, slow, reproach
[aʊ]	now, about, doubt
[ɛɚ]	air, care, there (AS)
[ɛəʳ]	air, care, there (RP & MA)
[ɪɚ]	ear, dear, here, tier (AS)
[ɪəʳ]	ear, dear, here, tier (RP & MA)
[ɔɚ]	pour, four, soar, o`er (AS)
[ɔəʳ]	pour, four, soar, o`er (RP & MA)
[ʊɚ]	sure, tour, poor (AS)
[ʊəʳ]	sure, tour, poor (RP & MA)
[ɑɚ]	are, heart, garden (AS)
[ɑəʳ]	are, heart, garden (RP & MA)

TRIPHTHONGS:

SYMBOL	KEY WORDS
[aɪɚ]	fire, choir, admire (AS)
[aɪəʳ]	fire, choir, admire (RP & MA)
[aʊɚ]	our, flower, tower (AS)
[aʊəʳ]	our, flower, tower (RP & MA)

ADDITIONAL SYMBOLS:

[']   A diacritical mark placed before a syllable that has primary stress.

[ˌ]   A diacritical mark placed before a syllable that has secondary stress.

[ɾ]   A flapped t or d. It is produced by flapping the tongue against the gum ridge. It is very characteristic of medial t's and d's in coloquial and southern American accents.

[ʔ]   A glottalized consonant, usually final or medial t's and d's. It is characteristic of conversational speech patterns in English. Ex: that day- thaʔ day   had done- haʔ done

[(ʊ)]   An off glide symbol. A weak extra vowel sounded after a primary vowel that is characteristic of certain Southern American accents.

GENERAL NOTES:

The texts in this guide have been transcribed into three primary pronunciations: American Standard, British Received and Mid-Atlantic Pronunciations. American Standard is a neutralized pronunciation of American English that is used for the American stage. British Received Pronunciation is an upper class pronunciation that is the performance standard for British works in the United Kingdom. Mid-Atlantic is a hybrid pronunciation that combines elements of both British and North American pronunciation. Some other variants found in this guide are for colloquial American or American Southern accents.

The standard performance practice for these arias was taken into consideration. The transcriptions were based on the character who sings them, the setting of the opera, and the geographic origin of the works. In general, if the composer and/or the text are North American, then the text is transcribed into American Standard pronunciation or one of the American variants. If the composer and or the text are British, then the text is transcribed into British Received Pronunciation. If the composer is North American but the text is British, then the text is transcribed into Mid-Atlantic. These are guidelines. The pronunciations can be modified to accommodate the production values of a specific operatic production or individual artistic taste.

52

THE MOTHER OF US ALL
music: Virgil Thomson
text: Gertrude Stein

What what is it
In American Standard Pronunciation:

ʍɑt ʍɑt ɪz ɪt
What what is it,

ʍɑt ɪz ɪt
what is it,

ʍɑt ɪz ðə fɔls ænd ðə tɹu
what is the false and the true

ænd aɪ seɪ tu ju ˈsuzən bi ˈænθəni
and I say to you Susan B. Anthony,

ju noʊ ðə fɔls fɹʌm ðə tɹu
you know the false from the true

ænd jɛt ju wɪl nɑt weɪt
and yet you will not wait.

ʍɛn maɪ aɪz ænd aɪ hæv aɪz
When my eyes, and I have eyes,

ʍɛn maɪ aɪz
when my eyes,

bɪˈjɑnd ðæt aɪ sik nɑʔ tu ˈpɛnɪˌtɹeɪt ðə veɪl
beyond that I seek not to penetrate the veil,

ʍaɪ ʃʊd ju wɑnt ʍɑt ju hæv ˈtʃoʊzən
why should you want what you have chosen,

ʍɛn maɪn aɪz
when mine eyes;

ʍaɪ du ju wɑnt ðæt ðə kɝˈtən meɪ ɹaɪz
why do you want that the curtain may rise,

ʍɛn maɪn aɪz
when mine eyes,

ʍaɪ ʃʊd ðə ˈvɪʒən bi ˈoʊpənd tu ʍɑt laɪz bɪˈhaɪnd
why should the vision be opened to what lies behind,

ʍaɪ ˈsuzən bi ˈænθəni faɪt ðə faɪt
why, Susan B. Anthony fight the fight

ðæt ɪz ðə faɪt ðæt ˈɛni faɪt
that is the fight, that any fight

meɪ bi ə faɪt fɔɹ ðə ɹaɪt
may be a fight for the right.

aɪ hɪɹ ðæt ju seɪ ðæt ðə wɝd meɪl
I hear that you say that the word male

ʃʊd nɑt bi ˈɹɪtən ˈɪntu ðə ˌkɑnstɪˈtuʃən
should not be written into the constitution

əv ðə juˈnaɪtɪd steɪts əv əˈmɛɹɪkə
of the United States of America,

bʌt aɪ seɪ
but I say,

ðæt soʊ lɔŋ ðæt ðə ˈgɔɚdʒəs ˈɛnsən əv ðə ɹɪˈpʌblɪk
that so long that the gorgeous ensign of the republic,

stɪl fʊl haɪ ædˈvænst
still full high advanced,

ɪts aɚmz ænd ˈtɹoʊfiz ˈstɹimɪŋ ɪn ðɛɚ oˈɹɪdʒɪnəl ˈlʌstɚ
its arms and trophies streaming in their original luster

nɑt ə stɹaɪp ɪˈɹeɪst ɔɚ pəˈlutɪd
not a stripe erased or polluted

nɑt ə sɪŋgəl staɚ əbskjʊɚd
not a single star obscured.

STREET SCENE

music: Kurt Weill
book: Elmer Rice
lyrics: Langston Hughes (based on the play by Elmer Rice)

Let things be like they always was
(Frank's Aria)

In Colloquial American Pronunciation:

lɛʔ	θɪŋz	bi	laɪk	ðeɪ	ɔlweɪz	waz
Let	**things**	**be**	**like**	**they**	**always**	**was,**

ðæts	gʊd	ɪˈnʌf	fɚ	mi
That's	**good**	**enough**	**for**	**me.**

lɛʔ	θɪŋz	əgɛn	bi	seɪf	æn	saʊnd
Let	**things**	**again**	**be**	**safe**	**and**	**sound,**

ðə	weɪ	ðeɪ	jus	tə	bi
The	**way**	**they**	**used**	**to**	**be.**

ʍɑts	goʊɪŋ	ɑn
What's	**going**	**on?**

ʍaɪ	ɪz	ɪt	soʊ	bæd
Why	**is**	**it**	**so**	**bad?**

ɪf	ju	æsk	mi
If	**you**	**ask**	**me,**

ðə	wɝld	ɪz	ˈgoʊɪŋ	mæd
the	**world**	**is**	**going**	**mad!**

lʊk	æt	ðiz	nu	ˈfæŋgəld	aɪˈdiəz	ˈgoʊɪŋ	ɹaʊnd
Look	**at**	**these**	**new**	**fangled**	**ideas**	**going**	**round,**

fɹi	lʌv	dɪˈvɔɚs	ænd	bɝθ	kənˈtɹoʊl
Free	**love,**	**divorce,**	**and**	**birth**	**control.**

jʌŋ	gɝlz	ˈsmoʊkɪn	ˌsɪgəˈɹɛts
Young	**girls**	**smoking**	**cigarettes,**

ðɛɚ	ˈdɹɛsɪz	ʌp	əˈɹaʊn	ðɛɚ	nɛks
Their	**dresses**	**up**	**around**	**their**	**necks,**

ænd	mɛn	ˈkʌmɪn	ɪn
And	**men**	**coming**	**in,**

ˈbɹeɪkɪn	ʌp	ˈdisənʔ	ˈpipəlz	hoʊmz
breaking	**up**	**decent**	**people's**	**homes.**

bʌʔ	ɪʔ	eɪnʔ	ˈgʌnə	bi	ðæʔ	weɪ	əˈɹaʊnd	hɪɚ
But	**it**	**ain't**	**gonna**	**be**	**that**	**way**	**around**	**here,**

ju	hɪɚ
You	**hear?**

ɪf	ˈɛniˈwʌn	ɪn	maɪ	haʊs	wants	ðæʔ	kaɪnd	əv	stʌf
If	**anyone**	**in**	**my**	**house**	**wants**	**that**	**kind**	**of**	**stuff,**

oʊ	noʊ
Oh	**no!**

maɪ kɪdz ɚ gʌnə bi bɹɔr ʌp ɹaɪt
My kids are gonna be brought up right!

nɑʔ ɹʌnɪn ðə stɹits æz ɪf ðɛɚ waɪld ɔl naɪt
Not running the streets as if they're wild all night.

ɪn ði oʊld deɪz ðeɪ dɪdənʔ kæɹɨ ɑn ðæʔ weɪ
In the old days they didn't carry on that way,

ænd aɪm ˈtɛlɪn ju ðeɪ eɪnʔ gʌnə du ɪʔ təˈdeɪ
And I'm telling you they ain't gonna do it today!

wɪð mi ðæʔ stʌf wɪl ˈnɛvɚ goʊ
With me that stuff will never go!

ɪn maɪ haʊs aɪ ɹʌn ðə ʃoʊ
In my house I run the show!

lɛʔ θɪŋz bi laɪk ðeɪ ˈɔlˈweɪz wɑz
Let things be like they always was,

ðæts gʊd ɪˈnʌf fɚ mi
That's good enough for me!

Note: Based on the length of the note value, sometimes the n of the "ing" can be dropped and sometimes it needs to be sounded as a full "ng".

ABOUT THE RUSSIAN IPA TRANSLITERATIONS
by David Ivanov

Following is a table of pronunciation for Russian diction in singing as transliterated in this volume. While the IPA is currently the diction learning tool of choice for singers not familiar with the foreign languages in which they sing, differences exist in transliterations, just as differences of pronunciation exist in the Russian language itself. Research from authoritative published sources as well as sensitivity to how the words interact with the music should guide the singer to the final result.

THE VOWELS

symbol	nearest equivalent in English	descriptive notes
[ɑ]	arm	
[ɛ]	met	
[i]	heat	
[o]	go	pure [o], not [oʊ]
[u]	put	
[ə]	about	
[ɨ]	not an English sound	pronounce as a throaty form of [i]

THE CONSONANTS

symbol	nearest equivalent in English
[b]	bank
[bʲ]	beautiful
[d]	dog
[dʲ]	adieu (French)
[f]	fat
[fʲ]	fume
[g]	gate
[gʲ]	legume
[k]	can
[kʲ]	cue
[l]	lot
[lʲ]	laugh
[m]	mat
[mʲ]	mule
[n]	not
[nʲ]	news
[p]	pin
[pʲ]	pure
[r]	flipped [r]
[rʲ]	flipped [r] in palatalized position
[s]	sat
[sʲ]	see
[t]	top
[tʲ]	costume
[v]	vat
[vʲ]	review
[x]	ach (German)
[xʲ]	not an English sound
[tʃ]	chair
[ʃtʃ]	mesh chair
[ʃ]	mesh
[ʒ]	measure

EUGENE ONEGIN

music: Pyotr Il'yich Tchaikovsky
libretto: Konstantin Shilovsky and Pyotr Il'yich Tchaikovsky (after a poem by Alexander Pushkin)

Lyubvi vse vozrasty kokorny
(Gremin's Aria)

lʲub ˈvʲi   fsʲɛ   vəz ras ˈti   pa ˈkor nɨ
Любви   **все**   **возрасты**   **покорны,**
To love   *all*   *ages*   *are submissive,*

ji ˈjo   pa ˈrɨ vɨ   blə gat ˈvor nɨ
её   **порывы**   **благотворны**
its   *impulses*   *are beneficial*

i   ˈju nə ʃi   v   ras ˈtsvʲɛ tʲə   lʲɛt
и   **юноше**   **в**   **расцвете**   **лет,**
both   *to a youth*   *in*   *blossoming*   *of age,*

jid ˈva   u ˈvʲi dʲif ʃɨ mu   svʲɛt
едва   **увидевшему**   **свет,**
(who) barely   *having seen the*   *world,*

i   zə ka ˈlʲo n:ə mu   sudʲ ˈboi
и   **закалнному**   **судьбой**
and   *hardened*   *by fate*

bai ˈtsu   s   sʲi ˈdo ju   gə la ˈvoi
бойцу   **с**   **седою**   **головой!**
warrior   *with*   *gray*   *head!*

a ˈnʲɛ gʲin   ja   skrɨ ˈvatʲ   nʲi   ˈsta nu
Онегин,   **я**   **скрывать**   **не**   **стану,**
Onegin,   *I*   *to conceal*   *won't*   *start,*

bʲi ˈzum nə   ja   lʲub ˈlʲu   tatʲ ˈja nu
безумно   **я**   **люблю**   **Татьяну!**
madly   *I*   *love*   *Tatiana!*

task ˈlʲi və   ʒiznʲ   ma ˈja   tʲik ˈla
Тоскливо   **жизнь**   **моя**   **текла,**
Drearily   *life*   *my*   *was flowing,*

a ˈna   ji ˈvʲi ləsʲ   i   da ˈla
она   **явилась**   **и**   **дала,**
she   *appeared*   *and*   *gave,*

kak   ˈson tsə   lutʃ   srʲi ˈdʲi   nʲi ˈnastʲ jə
как   **солнца**   **луч**   **среди**   **ненастья,**
like   *of sun*   *ray*   *in*   *foul weather,*

mnʲɛ   ʒiznʲ   i   ˈmo lə dəstʲ   da
мне   **жизнь**   **и**   **молодость,**   **да,**
to me   *life*   *and*   *youth,*   *yes,*

ˈmo lə dəstʲ   i   ˈstʃastʲ ji
молодость   **и**   **счастье!**
youth   *and*   *happiness!*

srʲi ˈdʲi   lu ˈka vɨx   məla ˈduʃnɨx
Среди   **лукавых,**   **малодушных,**
Amidst   *sly,*   *faint-hearted,*

ʃalʲ ˈnɨx   ba ˈlo və nːix   dʲi ˈtʲɛi
шальных   **балованных**   **детей,**
mad   *spoiled*   *children,*

zla ˈdʲɛ jif   i   smʲiʃ ˈnɨx
злодеев   **и**   **смешных,**
scoundrels   *and*   *absurd,*

i   ˈskuʃ nɨx
и   **скучных,**
and   *dull,*

tu ˈpɨx   prʲi ˈvas tʃi vɨx   su ˈdʲɛi
тупых,   **привязчивых**   **судей;**
obtuse,   *quick*   *judges;*

srʲi ˈdʲi   ka ˈkʲɛ tək   bə ga ˈmolʲ nɨx
среди   **какеток**   **богомольных,**
amidst   *coquettes*   *religious,*

srʲi ˈdʲi   xa ˈlopʲ jiv   dəb ra ˈvolʲ nɨx
среди   **холопьев**   **добровольных,**
amidst   *slaves*   *voluntary,*

srʲi ˈdʲi   fsʲid ˈnʲɛv nɨx   ˈmod nɨx   stsɛn
среди   **вседневных**   **модных**   **сцен,**
amidst   *everyday*   *stylish*   *scenes,*

utʃ ˈtʲi vɨx   ˈlas kə vɨx   iz ˈmʲɛn
учтивых,   **ласковых**   **измен;**
courteous,   *affectionate*   *betrayal;*

srʲi ˈdʲi   xa ˈlod nɨx   prʲi gaˈ vo rəf
среди   **холодных**   **приговоров**
amidst   *frigid*   *verdicts*

ʒɨs tə ka ˈsʲɛr dəi   su ji ˈtɨ
жестокосердой   **суеты,**
cruel-hearted   *vanity,*

srʲi ˈdʲi   da ˈsad nəi   pus ˈto tɨ
среди   **досадной**   **пустоты**
amidst   *annoying*   *emptiness*

ras ˈtʃo təf   dum
расчётов,   **дум**
calculations,   *thoughts*

i   rəz ga ˈvo rəf
и   **разговоров,**
and   *conversations,*

a ˈna   blʲis ˈta jit   kak   zvʲiz ˈda
она   **блистает,**   **как**   **звезда**
she   *shines,*   *like*   *star*

va   ˈmra kʲi   ˈno tʃi   v   ˈnʲɛ bʲi   ˈtʃis təm
во   **мраке**   **ночи,**   **в**   **небе**   **чистом,**
in   *gloom*   *of night,*   *in*   *sky*   *clear,*

i   mnʲɛ   jiv ˈlʲa jit sʲə   fsʲig ˈda
и   **мне**   **является**   **всегда**
and   *to me*   *appears*   *always*

f   si ˈjanʲ ji   ˈɑn gʲi lə
в   сияньи   ангела,
in   aureole   of angel,

f   si ˈjanʲ ji   ˈɑn gʲi lə   lu ˈtʃis təm
в   сияньи   ангела   лучистом!
in   aureole   of angel   radiant!

lʲub ˈvʲi   fsʲɛ   vəz rɑs ˈtɨ   pɑ ˈkor nɨ
Любви   все   возрасты   покорны,
To love   all   ages   are submissive,

ji ˈjo   pɑ ˈrɨ vɨ   blə gɑt ˈvor nɨ
её   порывы   благотворны
its   impulses   are beneficial

i   ˈju nə ʃi   v   rɑs ˈtsvʲɛ tʲə   lʲet
и   юноше   в   расцвете   лет,
both   to a youth   in   blossoming   of age,

jid ˈvɑ   u ˈvʲi dʲif ʃi mu   svʲet
едва   увидевшему   свет,
(who) barely   having seen the   world,

i   zə kɑ ˈlʲo nːə mu   sudʲ ˈboi
и   закалнному   судьбой
and   hardened   by fate

bɑi ˈtsu   s   sʲi ˈdo ju   gə lɑ ˈvoi
бойцу   с   седою   головой!
warrior   with   gray   head!

ɑ ˈnʲɛ gʲin   jɑ   skrɨ ˈvatʲ   nʲi   ˈstɑ nu
Онегин,   я   скрывать   не   стану,
Onegin,   I   to conceal   won't   start,

bʲi ˈzum nə   jɑ   lʲub ˈlʲu   tatʲ ˈjɑ nu
безумно   я   люблю   Татьяну!
madly   I   love   Tatiana!

tɑsk ˈlʲi və   ʒiznʲ   mɑ ˈjɑ   tʲik ˈlɑ
Тоскливо   жизнь   моя   текла,
Drearily   life   my   was flowing,

ɑ ˈnɑ   ji ˈvʲi ləsʲ   i   dɑ ˈlɑ
она   явилась   и   дала,
she   appeared   and   gave,

kɑk   ˈson tsə   lutʃ   srʲi ˈdʲi   nʲi ˈnɑstʲ jə
как   солнца   луч   среди   ненастья,
like   of sun   ray   in   foul weather,

mnʲɛ   ʒiznʲ   i   ˈmo lə dəstʲ   dɑ
мне   жизнь   и   молодость,   да,
to me   life   and   youth,   yes,

ˈmo lə dəstʲ   i   ˈstʃɑstʲ ji
молодость   и   счастье,
youth   and   happiness,

i   ʒiznʲ   i   ˈmo lə dəstʲ   i   ˈstʃɑstʲ ji
и   жизнь   и   молодость   и   счастье!
and   life   and   youth   and   happiness!